UNSTUFF

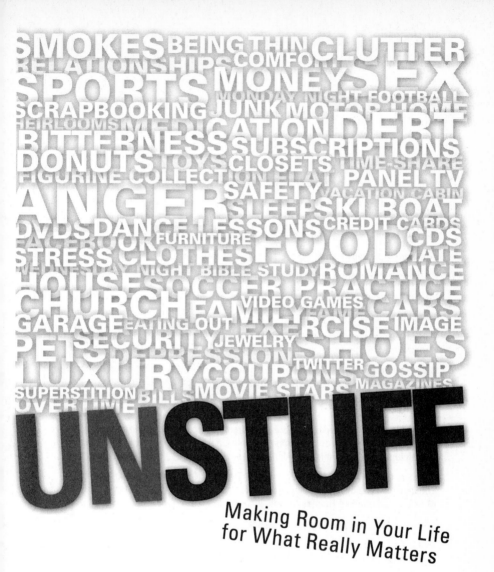

SMOKES BEING THIN CLUTTER
RELATIONSHIPS COMFO
SPORTS MONEY SEX
MONDAY NIGHT FOOTBALL
SCRAPBOOKING JUNK MOTOR HOME
HEIRLOOMS CATION DEBT
BITTERNESS SUBSCRIPTIONS
DONUTS TOYS CLOSETS TIME SHARE
FIGURINE COLLECTION PANEL TV
ANGER SAFETY VACATION CABIN
SLEEP SKI BOAT
DVDS DANCE LESSONS CREDIT CARDS
FURNITURE CDS
STRESS CLOTHES FOOD ATE
NIGHT BIBLE STUDY ROMANCE
HOUSE SOCCER PRACTICE
CHURCH FAMILY CARS
VIDEO GAMES
GARAGE EATING OUT RCISE IMAGE
PETS SECURITY JEWELRY SHOES
LUXURY COUPONS TWITTER GOSSIP
SUPERSTITION BILLS MOVIE STARS MAGAZINES
OVERTIME

UNSTUFF

Making Room in Your Life for What Really Matters

HAYLEY & MICHAEL DiMARCO

Tyndale House Publishers, Inc., Carol Stream, Illinois

Visit Tyndale's exciting Web site at www.tyndale.com.

Visit Hungry Planet's Web site at www.hungryplanetbooks.com.

TYNDALE and Tyndale's quill logo are registered trademarks of Tyndale House Publishers, Inc.

Unstuff: Making Room in Your Life for What Really Matters

Cover design and interior direction by Hungry Planet.

Interior designed by Beth Sparkman

Edited by Stephanie Voiland

Published in association with the literary agency of Yates & Yates, LLP, 1100 Town & Country Road, Suite 1300, Orange, CA 92868.

Library of Congress Cataloging-in-Publication Data

DiMarco, Hayley.
    Unstuff : making room in your life for what really matters / Hayley and Michael DiMarco.
        p. cm.
    Includes bibliographical references (p.   ).
    ISBN 978-1-4143-3478-3 (sc)
    1. Consumption (Economics)—Religious aspects—Christianity. 2. Christian life. 3. DiMarco, Michael. 4. DiMarco, Hayley. I. DiMarco, Michael. II. Title.
    BR115.C67D56 2010
    241'.68—dc22   2010036522

Printed in the United States of America

16   15   14   13   12   11   10
7   6   5   4   3   2   1

To the One who created all and knows our hearts.
May we worship you and not your creation
(or the creation's creations).

*Note: This is dedicated to God,
not Steve Jobs. Sorry for any confusion.*

CONTENTS

PRODUCT DISCLAIMER

This book was a spiritual struggle to write, mainly because we are both prone to consumerism. We look to stuff to give us joy, happiness, comfort, and peace. When we decided to investigate the role of giving—or the lack thereof—in our lives, we went all in, holding nothing back. We wanted to fully surrender to God's call, whatever that would mean for us. As we reflected on how we really lived our lives, we turned pale. We felt an overwhelming sense of shame and lost opportunity. And to be honest, **we sickened at the prospect of having to give up our love of stuff and the consumption of it**.

But the real shocker to us was the realization that *STUFF IS SO MUCH MORE THAN JUST THINGS YOU CAN BUY OR PHYSICALLY POSSESS.* Surprising as it sounds, it's actually possible to live a monastic lifestyle and still be sinning in relation to stuff. In these pages we share our shocking discovery of the massive implications stuff has on our physical, mental, and spiritual lives. Along the way we are discovering it's not how much stuff we have, but how we think about stuff and what we do with it that either positively or negatively affects our relationship with God.

We've heard the deeper you grow spiritually, the more sinful you get—not because you choose more sin, but because you start to recognize the sin already present in your life that you once were used to living with and joyfully (or ignorantly) accepted. While the study of truth is bound to open a few wounds and rip off a few scabs, we decided it was worth the pain to get to the bottom of the bondage of sin—in this case, the sin of "stuffing." So like taking a cheese grater to our rear ends, we turned our lives upside down, changing from gluttons to gluttons for punishment. **We've begun to Unstuff our lives so we can live more fully for God and for others.** In the process, we've made a few blunders, learned a few things, and made a lot of changes.

We hope you'll join us on this journey so that you, too, might discover what God has in store for you—how he wants you to relate to your stuff and how he wants to use your stuff as a help, not a hindrance, to advancing his Kingdom.

Our Stuff

There was a time when we got the sensation **we were drowning in our stuff**. We had more stuff than we had space to put it. We tripped over it, shoved it into spaces too small for it, shuffled it, hid it, garaged it.

We consider ourselves *CONSUMERS*. We like **supporting the local economy by purchasing much and often**. We're good at it—we find good deals, we make every effort to buy good stuff, and we congratulate ourselves on our excellent purchasing skills. When something breaks, we tend to buy another rather than fix the old. If we want it, we get it. We consume well and do our part to keep this economy of ours going. But the truth is, in our consumeristic lifestyle, *we had made idols of our stuff*.

We started to feel uneasy, stressed out by the very stuff we had sought to make us feel better. And we asked ourselves, *What's the point? Why so much stuff?* The uneasy feeling of having **so much but not having what we wanted** prompted us to do a thorough audit of our habits, closets, and entire lives.

Downsizing: Our Social and Spiritual Experiment in Unstuffing

As we discussed the need to Unstuff our lives, we brainstormed fantastic ways we could break free from the tyrannical hold our belongings had over us. In the process, **WE CAME UP WITH THIS HAREBRAINED IDEA TO DOWNSIZE.** The conversation went something like this:

Hayley: How big will it be?

Michael: Big enough.

Hayley: But how will we have room to work and do school and let Addy play?

Michael: We'll get something with enough space for all of us.

Hayley

A year ago, when Michael suggested that our family—the two of us and our daughter, Addy, who was three at the time—move into a two-hundred-square-foot motor home and live on the road for three months, I was simultaneously excited and freaked out. We'd been tired of the rat race for a while, and we wanted more out of life. Around the same time, we proposed a new project—a documentary featuring Bible readings and firsthand stories of homeless individuals across America. Michael could have done the tour alone, but we felt like it was a good opportunity for our whole family to Unstuff and to practice living for something more. All the "necessities" of life flew past my mind like farm animals in *The Wizard of Oz*. Part of me

was enamored of the romance of it all—hitting the
road with not much more than a prayer and a dream,
risking it all, and trusting God to provide as we
downsized our lives. I mean, I'm all for letting God
purify us through hard work, but I'm also all about
making it as painless as possible. Is that bad? So I
told Michael, "I'm a nester—I like things to be homey.
Will it be homey? Can I decorate?" And by decorate,
I meant *buy cute things to make it look cute*. I know,
how ironic that in our attempt to downsize, here I was
trying to acquire *more* stuff. So when I came home
with matching plastic dishes, place mats, and festive
tablecloths for indoor and outdoor meals, Michael
looked at me in disbelief and said, "Really? Which
part of Unstuffing don't you understand?" (Yes, he's
the gentle, sensitive one. . . .) See, for me, a shopper,
this *was* Unstuffing. I wasn't buying china; I was
buying plastic. I was shopping at Target, not Macy's.
See? Unstuffing. But alas, Michael was right. I was so
excited about the trip that I'd forgotten the reason
behind it. So back I went to Target to return all but the
essential purchases.

Michael

The idea of asking my wife to get by on less tore at my
provision muscle a bit. I want to make sure she has what
she needs, and I want her to be happy. But the more we
talked about things, the more we realized that for both
of us, happiness wasn't our ultimate goal (although in a
lot of unexpected ways, it was the outcome). Happiness,
it turns out, isn't always the best option for the life of
the believer. There are times when we have to deny
ourselves or our desire to be happy in order to reach a
greater spiritual purpose.

Once we'd decided for sure to take our family on the road for three months, I started looking at conversion vans as our best option. But the lack of a toilet perplexed my wife and would have significantly slowed down our drive. So I moved up to a Class C motor home. But the lack of space for us to both work and live simultaneously bothered us too. So before we knew it, we were moving in to a two-hundred-square-foot motor home with bunk beds for Addy and a separate door to the bedroom in the back. It was an amazing deal that we normally wouldn't have been able to afford, but it was right at the top of our budget. All was well . . . at first.

When we moved our family into a motor home for three months, **we learned a lot about necessity**. We could have only what we needed—there wasn't room for more. ***We had to live on less—less stuff and less space***—and it turned out we loved every minute of it. **Instead of making us crazy, for the most part it set us free.** We no longer felt distant and too busy to be with each other. We had no other choice but to be with each other. After all, there was not enough room to be apart! And there wasn't enough stuff to distract us from what really matters: family, love, and faith. In those months of living in close quarters with just a few of our things, we discovered a freedom we had never imagined.

unstuff.org

WHY UNSTUFF?

Did you ever think your life would be more than it is right now? Did you have visions of more success, more peace, more love, more comfort? If you aren't where you want to be yet, if there are things you still want to accomplish and experience, then you're normal. The desire for more isn't always a bad one. The longings for more hope, more peace, and more happiness are noble aspirations, and for the most part they are at the heart of our dreams for our future selves. Wanting more than you have today is normal, as the world defines it. It's how you get the "more" out of life that defines your success, regardless of whether you find what you imagined. ***But are you getting "more" of God in the process?***

This book is about taking a look at your life and all the stuff in it to determine if said stuff is making your life better or derailing it. Stuff, as we define it, can be just about anything: houses, furniture, cars, clothes, food, toys, or anything else you own. But it's also anything that consumes your time or demands your devotion: friends, church, thoughts, religion, Bible study, money, relationships, and those things that are designed to make your life better, more hopeful, and even more holy. **Stuff is essentially anything other than God.**

For the most part, *STUFF ISN'T INHERENTLY BAD OR GOOD; IT'S NEUTRAL.* It's what you think about it and what you do with it that affects the true success of your life and whether you are living it to the fullest. When Jesus came to earth, he said he came to give us "a rich and satisfying life" (John 10:10).

The Symptoms of Too Much Stuff

The truth is that most of us aren't as rich or as satisfied as we would like to be. There is never quite enough "rich and satisfying" to go around, is there? Most of us search for it in the stuff around us. We try to find fulfillment in our work, with our families, in our friendships. We try out new hobbies, collect new things, and purchase what we think will give us a glimpse of the full life that Jesus wants to give us, but it always seems to be just out of reach. **What we're really yearning for is the "more" of heaven** (or its main resident). It's as if it's written into our DNA—this knowledge that we don't quite have what was intended for us. And so we look the earth over for something to fill that need, something to quench that thirst.

Sometimes we find it—if only temporarily—in a new toy, a new experience, or a new love. We might get a glimpse of it in a shiny car or a flat-panel TV. Sometimes we taste it in a decadent meal or feel it in an amazing vacation destination. But when the flavor is gone and the sun has set, those old feelings of "not enough" return, or worse yet, the residual feelings of overindulgence drag us down. When we survey all that we've acquired or done and realize it has left us empty or bloated, *we get the hunch that something is missing* . . . and it's not more stuff. Stuff, though some is necessary for existence, isn't what gives us "a rich and satisfying life." That is found elsewhere, and it often takes some Unstuffing to get to the bottom of things.

If stuff is anything that isn't God, then the question is, **How do you know if you have too much stuff?** For believers, the answer must be when the stuff comes between us and God. Whether we like it or not, stuff has the tendency to occupy our minds. It gets us worked up, distracted, and focused on anything other than God. It demands our wallets, our clocks, and our hearts. It often requires our diligent protection and even our devoted worry and stress. The accumulation of stuff and the preservation of it can run us ragged.

If your life is poor—literally or mentally, socially, emotionally, or spiritually—then you'd be wise to look to your feelings about stuff for insight into why. *BOTH THOSE WHO HAVE MORE THAN ENOUGH AND THOSE WHO ARE IN NEED CAN BE SLAVES TO STUFF,* whether they're spending their thoughts and energy trying to attain more of it or trying to protect what they already have. Neither abundance nor lack is inherently evil. Both can, and should, be an opportunity for praise and thanksgiving (Philippians 4:11-13). Both are meant to lead us to where we

ASK YOURSELF ABOUT YOUR STUFF

What stuff can't you live without?
Of the things you mentioned, which are essential for life?
What stuff makes you feel better when you've had a bad day?
What is one thing you could never give away? Why?
What do you have too much of?
What about stuff stresses you out?
What stuff do you fear being without?
What stuff do you have to have in order to be happy and content?

need to be: a right relationship with God. Both show us something about his character and his provision. Both can teach us to rely on him no matter our circumstances, no matter what the world tells us. And out of both situations can come a richer and more satisfying life—provided we understand the purpose of stuff.

The Purpose of Stuff

Stuff was never meant to become a source of worry, fear, or obsession. It was never intended to occupy all our thoughts or suck up all our time. Stuff was meant to supply our needs. It was meant for good—for the good of the body and mind, soul and spirit. And that is what it is still meant for. The purpose of stuff is to contribute to our spiritual, mental, physical, and emotional well-being, not create emotional turmoil.

Jesus warns us about our tendency to get uptight about stuff. He knows we're human and acknowledges that there are things we need. But he also tells us that those are not things to obsess over or worry about.

> "That is why I tell you not to worry about everyday life—whether you have enough food and drink, or enough clothes to wear. Isn't life more than food, and your body more than clothing? Look at the birds. They don't plant or harvest or store food in barns, for your heavenly Father feeds them. And aren't you far more valuable to him than they are? Can all your worries add a single moment to your life? And why worry about your clothing? Look at the lilies of the field and how they grow. They don't work or make their clothing, yet Solomon in all his glory was not dressed as beautifully as they are. And if God cares so wonderfully for wildflowers that are here today and thrown

into the fire tomorrow, he will certainly care for you. Why do you have so little faith? So don't worry about these things, saying, 'What will we eat? What will we drink? What will we wear?' These things dominate the thoughts of unbelievers, but your heavenly Father already knows all your needs." MATTHEW 6:25-32

God says we don't have to get all worked up worrying about what stuff we have or don't have, but we can thank him for what we do have: food, clothing, and shelter. **The most basic purpose of stuff, then, is to meet our needs.** When we let stuff or the pursuit of stuff lead us to distraction—when stuff is the source of anything from worry to envy to depression—it has lost its purpose. And when we use stuff to meet any of the needs that God himself has promised to meet, it loses its purpose then, too. Sometimes in our abundance we give thanks to the stuff that surrounds us instead of thanking God for those things. We look to our possessions to supply us with hope, salvation, comfort, and peace. We lean on the stuff itself to meet our needs—needs that should lead us to the hand of the Father instead of to the door of Macy's or Best Buy.

When we perceive that we are lacking something or feel envy over what we don't have, we are essentially accusing God of deceit, of failing to come through on his promises. *He isn't providing*, we silently complain. And that is the beginning of all our unrest. We start to believe, if only in part, that God can't be trusted, that he won't do what he said he'd do, that the lilies are more important than his children and their needs. Stuff becomes a stumbling block to the heart that believes its needs are unmet. And in that moment, *WHEN THE PURPOSE OF STUFF GETS PERVERTED, UNSTUFFING IS IN ORDER.*

Stuff doesn't have to bring destruction or distraction, though.

If we look at and use it rightly, it can serve another purpose: to bring glory to God. It says so right there in Romans 11:36: "Everything comes from him and exists by his power and is intended for his glory." God's provision in the lives of believers is a witness to anyone looking that God can be trusted—that his Word is true and he won't neglect his kids. And it isn't so much our lack or our abundance that is the source of glory, but our God-given ability to be content with just what we have, right when we have it.

Life on the Road, Day 1

Hayley: How much stuff does a human being require? The answer to that has dramatically changed for me in the past three weeks. After loading the motor home with only what we need, I had the realization that I use more than I need every day. And the word *gluttony* came to mind. Is stuff bad for you? No, but how much more good could I do if stuff were no longer the focus of my life?

There is another purpose for stuff: it allows us to meet the needs of others. "You will be enriched in every way so that you can always be generous. And when we take your gifts to those who need them, they will thank God" (2 Corinthians 9:11). When we show generosity with what we have, it puts the spotlight right back on the one who made it all possible—the Giver of all good things.

Let's face it: to most of us, stuff feels good. Along our journey to Unstuffing, we've found that *unless we have some good reasons to stop accumulating stuff, we're just not going to do it*. As it turns out, there *are* a number of compelling reasons to Unstuff—some practical, some psychological, some spiritual. Here are our top eleven.

Reason #1: *to find more time*

When we downsized from our 3,200-square-foot house to a motor home, it took some adjusting. We couldn't bring everything we loved—not even the dog. We couldn't cook the way we liked to, we didn't have space to run, and we couldn't really even be alone, but we had each other. That three-month experience of living on less was the most rewarding and amazing experience we've ever had. Perhaps best of all, our family had more time for one another than ever before. Instead of cleaning and organizing, mowing and repairing, we spent time together. **Instead of playing with stuff and purchasing new stuff, we spent time together.** We were never far from each other, and we learned to appreciate the simplicity of a life with less.

We aren't advocating this as a model for everyone to follow. But for us, it served as an example of how much more time can be carved out for the important things like family and friends when there is less stuff to corral and manage. At the pace of life most of us keep, there is never enough time to do all we have to do. And so we speed things up—we cook faster, drive faster, eat faster, and work faster. We have high-speed Internet and speed dating. But *THE MORE THINGS SPEED UP, THE MORE WE CONSUME* and the less we truly enjoy life.

When we look at the life of Jesus, we don't see a man in a hurry. His pace allowed him to concentrate on what really mattered—people. We have to wonder: what would it be like if Jesus walked the earth today? Maybe this generation wouldn't have time for him. Maybe we wouldn't even notice him because our pace is so hurried, our calendars are so crowded, and our attention spans are so short. When we let the stuff in our lives steal time from us, our focus strays from the God we serve and lands squarely on the stuff that was meant to serve us. If time gets away from you, it might be time to consider how much you give the stuff in your life.

TIME TAKERS

What stuff do you spend most of your time on? Consider keeping a time journal: for one week write down every activity you do and how much time it takes. You might want to include categories, such as the following:

- Sleeping
- Eating
- Preparing food
- Working
- Driving
- Cleaning
- Caring for children
- Playing
- Praying
- Studying
- Exercising
- Making household repairs
- Shopping
- Organizing
- Talking with friends
- Attending church
- Spending time with spouse
- Spending time with kids
- Participating in a hobby

Fill in the amount of time you spend on each item and then take a look at it objectively. Do you have enough time for what matters in your life? Are you happy with what gets most of your time, or are there things you would like to change? If you didn't have to spend so much time and effort paying for, maintaining, and cleaning your stuff, would you have more time for other things that are more important to you?

Reason #2: *to put an emphasis on people*

When our minds are set on stuff, it can be easy to give people a backseat in our lives. We forget that stuff breaks, gets old, rusts, and wears out, but relationships grow and strengthen. They are vehicles God uses to teach us more about ourselves and about himself.

We both grew up in the Northwestern United States, a rainy and muddy place. Because of that, many homes there were built with mudrooms—places where shoes and raincoats come off so the rest of the house will stay clean. So when we had our own home, we had to decide if we wanted to embrace the custom of asking visitors to remove their shoes before entering.

Life on the Road, Day 2

Hayley: Okay, going to the mall is a totally different experience now that we're on the road. As I walked by the stores, I was relaxed for the first time ever in a mall setting. Instead of looking in windows like a hawk for the "perfect thing," I enjoyed just being with my family. I knew we had no space to put any more stuff, so my mind wasn't on purchasing but just being. Because of that, **a whole new world opened up for me, and the stress and pull of bargain shopping was gone.** Suddenly I wasn't running into each store to try things on or to check prices—my family was getting all my energy and time. I learned that downsizing your possessions is one thing; downsizing your appetite is even more amazing.

It keeps the carpet clean, we told ourselves. But **the truth is that it put our concern for our stuff over our concern for people**.

There was a time when women would cover their furniture in plastic in order to protect it from people who might soil it. The sensation of sitting on plastic isn't a pleasant one. The subtle message is that there's a higher value placed on stuff than on people. Fortunately, this fad has gone out of style, but there are many similar trends that a lot of us hold to. Like having decor or entire rooms in the house that are off limits to kids because we're sure they would mess things up, break them, or otherwise ruin them. Intentional or not, this sends the message, *Our stuff is more valuable than you are, so stay away from it.*

Life on the Road, Day 3

Michael: Today our life is dramatically different from a week ago. The pressure of moving our house from town to town across the United States and figuring out all the systems on the RV is daunting for me. Whose bright idea was this? But while I work, my daughter plays at my feet. When I eat, she sits across the table from me. As we talk, we know that we will be together in this small space for the next three months, and the idea excites me. It also scares me. I need my space, my time. But that isn't possible now, and I'm starting to think that this is just what I need. Side note: It seems Hayley is fond of having hot water. Will shower in the campground showers from now on.

CAN YOU IMAGINE JESUS OBSESSING ABOUT PEOPLE GETTING DUST ON HIS ROBE? Can you see him focusing his time and energy collecting stuff, cleaning stuff, and arranging stuff? Obviously that's ridiculous. But it might be worth considering whether the stuff in your life has affected your relationships.

Reason #3: *to focus on the good stuff*

Those who Unstuff have the opportunity to shift their focus from what will soon go out of style, break, or otherwise become useless and put it onto the things that really matter. As believers, we should have clear values: to prioritize love, service, and kindness, and to cherish eternal things. But when we get our focus out of whack, we lose sight of what's most important. When a family takes the opportunity to Unstuff their lives, they have more energy to devote to things that really matter. **Kids don't**

TIME AND VALUES

Take a look at the following list and identify your top five values. Do you have time to practice and live out the life you believe in, or are you too consumed by all the stuff?

- Family
- Service
- Generosity
- Patience
- Fellowship
- Study
- Charity
- Joy
- Compassion
- Prayer
- Peace
- Marriage
- Love
- Honesty
- Worship
- Simplicity
- Community
- Rest
- Self-control
- Hospitality

really want more stuff; they want mentorship and more relationship.

If you were to take an inventory of your life and set the things you value most against the reality of how you live, where would you say your focus is? Has your focus been shifted onto things that are less important?

Reason #4: *to form more heavenly attachments*

> "Don't store up treasures here on earth, where moths eat them and rust destroys them, and where thieves break in and steal. Store your treasures in heaven, where moths and rust cannot destroy, and thieves do not break in and steal. Wherever your treasure is, there the desires of your heart will also be." MATTHEW 6:19-21

There is a spiritual angle to all this talk about stuff. The way we think about stuff and deal with the accumulation of it will play a part in determining our level of spiritual growth and peace. *Unstuffing is the only way to rid ourselves of our earthly attachments so we can form more heavenly ones.* As Jesus put it, we can't serve two masters (Matthew 6:24). Stuff can easily become a master when it leads us to do the opposite of what God would have us do—in other words, when it leads us to sin. When stuff leads to worry, fear, stress, discontentment, lack of self-control, jealousy, envy, greed, and the list goes on, well, then, we've arrived at "Hello, master, how can I serve you?"

> "Since you have been raised to new life with Christ, set your sights on the realities of heaven, where Christ sits in the place of honor at God's right hand. Think about the things of heaven, not the things of earth." COLOSSIANS 3:1-2

God's Word calls us not to think about things of earth but the things of heaven. After all, that's where Jesus is, and that's where we are all headed. **The truth is that the world's value of stuff is reversed in heaven.** What's up is down, and what's down is up, so to speak. The world awards a person's value based on their accomplishments and accumulation. Here on earth, wealth signifies success, but in heaven it is humility and selflessness.

When you Unstuff your life, you take your focus off this world and put it onto heaven, where you can store up treasure that won't rust and that moths won't eat.

Reason #5: *to be set apart*

> "Come out from among unbelievers, and separate yourselves from them, says the LORD." 2 CORINTHIANS 6:17

> American households waste a total of $43 billion worth of food each year. Americans spend $12 billion on coffee per year. The average American wedding costs $26,327.[1]

Stuff surrounds us, and it's only increasing. Advertisements tout its value; people we idolize live out the illusion that stuff will fulfill you. *SUCCESS, MONEY, TOYS, TRINKETS, FINERY—THEY ALL PULL AT OUR HEARTS AND CALL US TO JOIN IN THE STUFF-FEST.* For the average person who doesn't have a spiritual eye on heaven, it's easy for them to assume that their possessions determine their value. In the movie *Confessions of a Shopaholic*, journalist and compulsive liar Rebecca Bloomwood finds herself some $16,000 in debt and trying to get back control of her life. At her Shopaholics Anonymous support group, however, she quickly falls back into adoration of shopping and the high it gives anyone who loves stuff. When it's her turn to share her addiction, she says, "I like shopping. Is there anything so wrong with that? I mean, stores are put there to enjoy. The experience is enjoyable, more than enjoyable—it's beautiful. The sheen of silk draped across a mannequin. The smell of new Italian leather shoes. The rush you feel when you swipe your card and it's approved and it all belongs to you. The joy you feel when you've bought something and it's just you and the shopping—all you have to do is hand over the little card. Isn't it just the best feeling in the world? . . . You feel so confident and alive, and happy and more!"

Our culture advocates that we continually strive for more and better, but we are called to be different. **To Unstuff is to set yourself apart.** The world finds it hard to conceive of self-denial for the sake of a greater good. But as believers, we have an example of self-denial in God himself, who was rich but became poor for our sakes (2 Corinthians 8:9). It is through him (and not our stuff) that we can have a rich and satisfying life.

Reason #6: *to learn surrender*

"Their first action was to give themselves to the Lord and to us, just as God wanted them to do." 2 CORINTHIANS 8:5

Surrender: To give yourself up to the power of someone

When you are at war, surrender is not a good thing. It signals the end of hope for all you were fighting for. It means waving the white flag and walking out with arms raised—battle over, but not won. But there is a surrender that brings you more victory than any battle or war ever could, and that's a surrender of your will and desires. In a spiritual sense, surrendering is not giving up but giving in to something far more powerful than yourself. Surrender is at the heart of faith. **Without a surrendered will, there is no faith in the first place.** But surrender doesn't stop at the point of conversion—it's a continual process as we learn to surrender our will with all its worldly desires to the will of one who is greater and knows more than we do. Surrender allows God to be in control, trusting that he's got it all figured out. Surrender is the doorway to freedom—freedom from the fight. When a surrendered heart no longer enters into the competition of life, it is free to focus on more important and eternal things. Jesus puts it this way: "If you try to hang on to your life, you will lose it" (Matthew 16:25). How counterintuitive is that? How can holding on to something assure its loss? Think of it this way: when you are clinging to a bunch of stuff, pulling it all tightly to your chest, you can no longer reach out. You can't hold any more than what you are carrying. But what you can hold in your hands is of little value in eternity. But when you surrender all your stuff—your things, your activities, your money, your relationships, and your plans—to God, you find yourself unencumbered by this world. You're free to serve and to do whatever God calls you to do. And suddenly there's no more struggle, no more battle within yourself that has to be won.

> "If you give up your life for my sake, you will save it."
> MATTHEW 16:25

Hayley

The thought of giving not from my abundance but from my poverty hurts. It makes my head spin and my stomach sick. I can fathom such a noble act only in my head but not in my heart. My heart clings with a white-knuckled grip to my ideals of the perfect life on earth. For as long as I can remember, I've lived with the notion that stuff will make me happy—that when I get older and more successful, I will have a bigger, newer house, own a new car, buy whatever I want, and finally be content in my perfect life.

But now I'm finding out this is the lie of the enemy; it's nothing more than the mantra of my idol. The American dream—the ideal of improvement, success, owning more, and therefore being more—could it have been wrong all along? How could I get this far in my faith and not know that my idol has been so systemically eating away at me? Every aspect of my life is wrapped up in the pursuit of more stuff while simultaneously trying to seek more of God and his grace.

Though I am disgusted by my idol of all these years, I cringe at the thought of saying good-bye. I'm gripped with the fear of the unknown and also with an uncanny resentment that I would have to figure this out right now, when I'm finally poised to be able to afford the house I've always dreamed of and fill it with the things I've always wanted. Why now? Why couldn't I have figured out this calling after I got a taste of what I've always dreamed of? Couldn't I just put this idea on pause and get back to it after I've already gotten the things I want? These are stupid questions, I know. The first step, they say, is to admit you have a problem. And I do have a problem: the love of stuff.

I have to acknowledge the irony. I am an idolater who wants to be free but fears a life without my little god.

Reason #7: *to find contentment*

"True godliness with contentment is itself great wealth."
1 TIMOTHY 6:6

It's not those of us who have nothing but those of us who wish for more who are poor. For many of us in the Western world, poverty is a state of mind and spirit. **Discontentment comes from deciding that what God has given us isn't enough.** It's a way of thinking that says, *Ha! God must have been lying when he told me* *that he would never forsake me and that he'd always provide for my needs* (Hebrews 13:5; Matthew 6:32-33).

But contentment can be yours if you are willing to Unstuff yourself. When you do, you take away the power of stuff in your life—the power that encourages you to become disgruntled and irritable when you don't get what you want or what you think you need. Contentment is not necessarily a matter of having exactly what you asked for but appreciating just what you have. You have wealth in your life that is just waiting to be uncovered, and it won't require a raise in salary or a higher credit score, but a choice—*A CHOICE TO MAKE STUFF UNIMPORTANT AND TO MAKE GOD ALL-IMPORTANT.*

Reason #8: *to gain self-control*

"Be earnest and disciplined in your prayers." 1 PETER 4:7

DO YOU LACK SELF-CONTROL?

When you have the chance to eat your favorite food, do you eat until it's all gone or until you're full?

When you are upset, hurt, or angry, do you impulsively let people know it?

When you are exhausted, do you have a pastime or practice you credit with renewing your strength?

When you are tempted, do you have an escape plan?

When you have to do something you don't want to do or want to do but have trouble following through on, do you put it off as long as possible?

When you really want to do something that's bad for you, do you rationalize that it's okay to do it just this once?

Is there any area in your life where you lack self-control? Since self-control, or the lack thereof, has to do with stuff—buying and not buying, eating and not eating, drinking and not drinking, spending and not spending—it stands to reason that Unstuffing has some kind of effect on self-control. Practice self-control, and you gain more self-control. It's like weight lifting: the more you lift, the more you're able to lift.

When you Unstuff, you give yourself a chance to practice self-control, and each area of your life that you Unstuff is gradually transformed.

Reason #9: *to become a giver*

> "Clean the inside by giving gifts to the poor, and you will be clean all over." LUKE 11:41

One of the things about stuff is that it can make you feel unclean, bloated, and, well, overstuffed. But Jesus offers a recipe for cleaning yourself up in Luke 11:41. The action takes place when the Pharisees invite Jesus to dine with them. They are aghast when he doesn't perform the ceremonial washing before he eats, which was Jewish custom. In response to their disdain, he points out how obsessed people can be about looking good on the outside when the inside is really what matters. He goes on to say that the way to clean up the inside is simply this: "Clean the inside by giving gifts to the poor, and you will be clean all over." Part of the Unstuffing process includes throwing out and selling, but it also includes cleaning up your life by giving. When you spend less on yourself, you have more to spend on those in need. When you downsize your stuff, you have the chance to upsize someone less fortunate. As pastor *Ray Ortlund Jr. frequently challenges his congregation, we are to think of our abundance as the debt we owe to those who are in need*. Proverbs 3:27 (ESV) says, "Do not withhold good from those to whom it is due, when it is in your power to do it." An alternate translation of the Hebrew renders it this way: "Do not withhold good from its owners. . . ."

In other words, **if we have abundance of something— whether it's talent, material possessions, money, or time—we're not really the ones who own it**. In God's eyes, its owners are those in need of it. Giving is a characteristic of holiness and of God himself, who didn't hold anything back from his children, not even the life of his Son.

Giving is valuable not only to the recipient but to the giver as well, because giving gets you outside of yourself and puts your thoughts on the things of God and the needs of his children. *WHEN YOU GIVE, GOD TAKES THOSE THINGS YOU'VE BEEN GIVEN AND INCREASES THEIR VALUE.* If you are controlled by fear and think you won't have enough left for yourself if you give first, then it's time to Unstuff—to get to the heart of the matter and open yourself up to the work of God in your life.

When we are willing to empty ourselves, to give beyond what's comfortable, we are available to be filled with what only God can give. Then we will be able to say, as David said, "My cup overflows with blessings" (Psalm 23:5).

Reason #10: *to love*

"Christ's love controls us." 2 CORINTHIANS 5:14

Andrew Murray put it like this: *"THE ABUNDANT LIFE . . . IS NOTHING LESS THAN THE FULL JESUS HAVING THE FULL MASTERY OVER OUR ENTIRE BEING, THROUGH THE POWER OF THE HOLY SPIRIT."* Unless Jesus has full mastery over you and all your stuff, you cannot say that Christ's love controls you. If there is stuff in your life that isn't under your control or the control of Jesus himself, you cannot say that Christ's love controls you.

Since God is the author and instructor of love, we know that we can only truly love when Christ's love controls us. In 2 Corinthians 5:14-15, Paul says, "Since we believe that Christ died for all, we also believe that we have all died to our old life. He died for everyone so that those who receive his new life will no longer live for themselves. Instead, they will live for Christ, who died and was raised for them." **Unstuffing teaches us to stop living for ourselves and to love others the way Christ loves them.** If we want more Christ in our lives, more of his love, then we must be willing to Unstuff the areas that are overstuffed.

Reason #11: *to grow your faith*

> "Because of their unbelief, he couldn't do any miracles among them except to place his hands on a few sick people and heal them. And he was amazed at their unbelief."
> MARK 6:5-6

In what areas do you lack faith? Is there a part of you, maybe even a secret part, where you don't trust God? In our search for a shortcut or an easier path to faith, a lot of times we look for stuff to provide the same results as genuine faith. And sometimes it does a decent job for a time—until it is taken away, ruined, or lost. Then its value to us is gone, and where does that leave us? *When the faith that should be in God is placed elsewhere, our doubts about his ability to provide and protect begin to infiltrate our hearts.* But when you practice Unstuffing and letting go of stuff's grip in your heart and soul, your faith grows in ways you could never have imagined.

Your Stuff List

Before we dive into the rest of the book, let's all take a quick inventory of stuff.

Lack or Abundance?

In the first column, write all the stuff you lack in your life. Write all the stuff you have an abundance of in the abundance column. After you make your lists, go back through each entry and write whether each is a godly thing (G) or an earthly thing (E).

Stuff I Lack	G or E	Stuff I Have in Abundance	G or E

After you complete the exercise, take a bird's-eye look at all your stuff and especially at the difference between what you have and what you want to have. **Look closely at all the earthly things and ask yourself why you want more of each one.** What are the spiritual or emotional ramifications of those desires? Then look at all the godly desires and see if there is a conflict with your earthly desires that is keeping you from achieving them.

The truth is that you can have some of the stuff some of the time, but you can't have all of the stuff all of the time. And the more stuff there is in your life, the less room for what really matters.

some final stuff

If you were truly free of all worry and concern for the stuff in your life, what do you think your life would look like? Would you find more time for long walks, for naps with the one you love, or for quiet moments of worship with your God? ***STUFF THAT ENCUMBERS YOU AND DOESN'T BRING YOU CLOSER TO THE ONE WHO CREATED YOU NEEDS TO BE UNSTUFFED.*** Unstuffing doesn't mean getting rid of everything you own and living a monastic life. It isn't about cruel deprivation of yourself and your family. The empty life isn't necessarily the fuller life. So Unstuffing doesn't have to do with getting rid of it all, but it does have to do with changing your relationship with stuff. For some it might mean selling everything you own and moving into a single-wide. For others it might mean reassessing what you have and finding out how it could benefit others around you.

Or you might be like the family in the film *The Blind Side*. This story, based on the life of pro football player Michael Oher and his adoptive family, is an amazing example of how your "much" can be used to move others from nothing to everything. In the story, the Tuohy family brings a homeless teenager to live in their home in an extraordinary act of compassion and love. Michael had been taken from his drug-addicted mother at the age of seven and moved from foster family to foster family until as a teenager he found himself alone and living on the street. He had received a scholarship to a Christian school in Memphis based on his athletic ability, but that only gave him a place to stay during the day—at night he was still on his own. But when the Tuohy family found him wandering the streets, they invited him home with them. From there they clothed him, gave him a place to belong, made him part of their family, and fought for him when the system seemed set on bringing him down. This amazing boy, neglected for so many years, began to flourish. In one especially amazing scene he tells Leigh Anne Tuohy, "I've never had one before." "What, a room to yourself?" she asks. "A bed," he replies. But the most unexpected and touching part about the Michael Oher story isn't the generous acts of his adoptive family but the relationship between them and **how much it impacted** not only the abandoned child but also *the family who reached out to him*.

When we give, we get more than we ever imagined. It isn't a measurable return, like money or gold, but an unfathomable return that offers us a life that is rich and satisfying, just as God intended.

In a recent conversation with our four-year-old daughter, we heard these words from her: *"I DO WHAT DIFFERENT DOES."* It was an interesting turn of phrase from such a young mind, and it got us thinking. If normal is acquisition, consumption, and unease at our own need for more, then isn't it best to be different? "Normal" carries with it debt, worry, stress, and isolation, but different takes an alternative view. It sees the need around us rather than within us. It trusts while others panic. It believes while others doubt. It gives while others hoard. So our hope is that you will be willing to do what different does, and we pray that we can shed some light as you take the journey toward Unstuffing your life.

COMFO
MONEY
MONDAY NIGHT FOOTB
JUNK MOTOR HO
CATION
SUBSCRIPTION
CLOSETS TIME-SHA
PANEL
SAFETY VACATION
SLEEP SKI BO
SSONS CREDIT CAR
URE FOOD
ES
BLE STUDY ROMAN
CER PRACTI
VIDEO GAMES
MILY CAR
RCISE IMA
JEWELRY SHOE
SION
COUPONS TWITTER GOSS
MAGAZI

WALLET STUFF

STUFF

Section One

unstuff.org

The Parable of Three Gardens

Three families each decided to plant a garden. "God has given us this extra space, so to be good stewards, let's plant a garden," they all said. So each family planted a beautiful garden. The first family said, "This garden is going to be great for our family. We'll save so much money on food." And they had more vegetables than they knew what to do with. They ate some, froze some, and canned some. But still there was more in the garden. So they looked out at all they had left and said, "God has given us such an abundance! We have more than we need, and we saved so much money." And they thanked the Lord.

The second family grew a garden with just as much produce—and more. When they had eaten all they could, frozen some, and canned some, they decided to gather all the extra into boxes and put it out in front of the house with a sign saying "Free for all." *Our abundance can become the abundance of others*, they thought.

The third family had just as fertile a garden, and when they had eaten all they could, frozen some, and canned some, they said, "Look at all that's left! It's enough to feed a lot more people, and I bet our neighbors have just as much surplus." And so this family went around to everyone in the neighborhood who had a garden and asked if they could collect their surplus for a local food bank that helped those in need. "Rather than let all this food go to waste, why don't we give the abundance God has given us to others who have not seen so much?"

The first family took advantage of space, and in doing so, they took care of their family as good stewards of what God had given them. The second family not only took care of their own finances and family but also helped others in the neighborhood. And the third family provided for even more in need by finding ways to give out of their abundance.

◆　　◆　　◆

"All too quickly the message is crowded out by the worries of this life, the lure of wealth, and the desire for other things, so no fruit is produced." MARK 4:19

"The love of money is the root of all kinds of evil. And some people, craving money, have wandered from the true faith and pierced themselves with many sorrows." 1 TIMOTHY 6:10

Most of the time we think of *stuff* as the things we buy and then consume or accumulate. But there are those who make money itself stuff. Usually we think of the fat cats on Wall Street or people named Scrooge when we think of obsession with money. But this inordinate love for cash isn't limited to the rich. It also affects middle-class Christians, making it too painful for us to give away our money to charitable causes or to the church. It can lead a family who could make it financially on one income to feel compelled to have both parents work full-time. However, **money was never meant to garner such affection, to become an idol or a passion**. If you love money, then you have found a sign that your life needs to be Unstuffed.

The opportunity to Unstuff is the opportunity to

clear out whatever has come between you and God. If
there is a part of you that is distracted, wandering, or distant from
him, chances are it's because of your stuff. And wallet stuff is one
of the biggest culprits keeping us focused on this world and all its
charms instead of on what's really important.

Maybe you know them—the Joneses. They are an imaginary
family that lives next door or just down the street from you. They
are the ones with the bigger house, the nicer car, and the better
life. They laugh a lot, travel a lot, buy a lot, and do a lot. There
seems to be no end to their success and happiness. They have it
made—or at least they have it more made than you, and you want
some of what they've got. **Keeping up with the Joneses is a
daunting task though.** Their life seems so magical, so perfect
that you never seem to get anywhere near it. By comparison, you
are stressed out, exhausted, living from paycheck to paycheck,
and never able to get ahead. You might manage to accumulate
something comparable to what the Joneses have, and even if it's a
cheaper knockoff from Target or Walmart, at least you've got a simulation of luxury. But the more you collect and the harder you work,
the more bloated and sluggish your life starts to feel. You only get
more stressed out, and you begin to realize that what you thought
would bring you happiness is really nothing but wood, fabric, metal,
and brick.

Deep inside, most of us are certain that other people have
it better than we do. As King Solomon in all his wisdom put
it, *"MOST PEOPLE ARE MOTIVATED TO SUCCESS BECAUSE THEY
ENVY THEIR NEIGHBORS. BUT THIS, TOO, IS MEANINGLESS—
LIKE CHASING THE WIND"* (Ecclesiastes 4:4). As human beings,
we tend to examine the external evidence to determine other
people's happiness and figure that if we could surround ourselves with the same stuff they have, we could be as happy and
successful as they are. And so we purchase. We accumulate. We

pay out in hopes of gaining a return, and that return is our much-hoped-for happiness, comfort, and peace. In Mark 4, Jesus talks about this concept of keeping up with the Joneses in the parable of the farmer sowing seeds in different soils. He tells his listeners that there are thorns that choke out his message of true hope. Those thorns, as he puts it, are "the worries of this life, the lure

Hayley

I know the sensation of getting choked by wallet stuff all too well. See, I'm a shopaholic—a recovering one, but once a shopaholic, always a shopaholic. In other words, I'm addicted to what we call stuffing—gathering stuff and bringing it into our home/life with the goal of making myself happy. The high I get from finding the perfect this or that is unparalleled. There is this dream, this little play that starts to take place in my mind as I hold all my "finds" close to my chest and walk toward the checkout. It feels like all is well in life—or soon will be. In my mind, owning this particular item will mean that I have arrived at my destination of the perfect life, or at least I'll be one step closer.

But a funny thing happens on the way to perfection, and that is the realization that purchasing stuff is like driving off a car lot: whatever you buy decreases in not just actual value but emotional value by at least 50 percent as soon as it becomes something you own instead of something you want. Sure, that thing might have value in that it meets a need or brings you some measure of joy, but over time that joy diminishes. The cushions wear out and start sagging, the color goes out of style, the model becomes outdated when the next generation comes out six months later. Your high goes out the door, and suddenly you need something else to give you another high.

of wealth, and the desire for other things" (verse 19). In other words, stuff. Stuff makes some big promises; it draws us in like a seasoned seducer of the heart. And so we pursue it with all our energy, sure it will give us all it says it will. But true fulfillment never follows.

We've done it all, we've bought it all, **we've given in to the urge to splurge**. We've enjoyed it for a time and then said, "Isn't it time to replace that?" Or "I'm so sick of that color." There was a time when a family would furnish a house once or buy one car, and then they were done. There were no upgrades that needed to be made. The furniture was going to last as long as they did; the car was going to be the only car they needed (hey, cars used to only come in black!), and life could be set on things other than accumulation. But now technology has advanced, stuff has become more disposable, merchandise gets better marketing hooks, and we're bombarded by news about sale prices. Our family is not immune to this condition. We have been known to buy a new couch every three or four years, not out of greed but out of "necessity"—the "need" to redecorate or keep up with the Joneses or take advantage of a good deal. We confess that at the beginning of this book project, we owned five cars (for three drivers—the two of us plus Hayley's mom), one motor home, and five TVs. So we're not writing this book from the perspective of people who can't hold a job so they are forced to embrace a monastic lifestyle. We know what it's like to be stuffers. As of late, however, we have been assessing our stuff in an attempt to determine not only its value but its destructiveness.

Yep, **we understand stuffing**. But it's because we understand it so well that we are writing this book. Wallet stuff is all about consumption and trying to use things to bring us happiness. When we look to things to provide what only God himself can produce in us (Galatians 5:22-23), we make a big mistake.

Hayley

A couple of years ago I began to have the nagging feeling of overstuffing, or stuffication, as I call it. One day I looked in my closet and felt sick. All those beautiful clothes that had once given me such a high were now not only boring but out of fashion and ugly. *What was I thinking?* I asked myself. My closet was bloated, spewing out blouses and jackets. My floor was covered with enough shoes to last me—and my five best friends—a lifetime, and I still could never find anything to wear. There was never "a place for everything and everything in its place" because all the places were too full. And at that point I said, "Enough!" And so I got radical. Now you might not want to try this at home, but this is what Michael and I did: we decided to give away, sell, or throw out ten things a day, every day. Sound impossible? Well, we did too, but it wasn't. This went on for an entire month, and still there was more stuff. It was a wake-up call to realize just how much we consume.

Reading the Signs

You may have never given your stuffing a second thought, but it just may be the cause of your spiritual malaise or the distance you feel from God.

When you get sick, do you ever try to figure out what's wrong with you by using one of those online health sites? You fill in your symptoms and hit Go, and then you wait to see all the things that could possibly be wrong with you. These sites can't know for sure the cause of your symptoms, but at least they give you a place to start. So you look through all the illnesses to see which one seems to fit your current condition. And based on that information, you can usually make some kind of a guess that at least helps you determine if you need to go to the doctor, the drugstore, or the mortuary.

Michael

I recently noticed that I have a Best Buy stockroom in
our basement, which is also home to the offices of our
company, Hungry Planet. There's almost one thousand
square feet of office space filled with laptops, video
equipment, and audio equipment, all gathering dust
in the graveyard of someone who's a tech reviewer
and early adopter. And while this technology had once
been useful in helping me keep up with the trends
and habits of the wired generation we write for, all the
excess was starting to make me sick. And so I started
to trash, sell, and give away my stockpile of gadgets
and tech stuff. In fact, when an author Hayley and I
really didn't know that well complained over Facebook
that her laptop was failing at the worst time, we sent
her one. I was beginning to find a way to redirect my
stuffing impulse and channel it to bless someone else
instead.

WAYS TO TELL IF YOU USE SHOPPING AS THERAPY

Do you ever buy more than will meet your basic needs?
Do you feel like your home is cluttered?
Do you run out of places to put things?
When a big-ticket item breaks, do you buy a new one rather than
    having it repaired?
Are you in debt?
Do you live paycheck to paycheck?
Are you a shopaholic?
Do you carry a balance on more than one credit card?

If you answered yes to one or more of these questions, then you
have a stuffing problem. If your life is feeling the effects of wallet
stuff, then it's time to Unstuff.

Well, when it comes to wallet stuff, you can make the same kind of discovery about yourself. **This book will offer a list of symptoms or signs to examine.** If any of these resonate with you, don't look at it as a bad thing but as a red flag to clean up your life and the stuff that comes between you and God. No one can Unstuff your life for you. Each of us has to take a sober look at ourselves to see what kinds of things entangle us to the point that we're barely keeping our nostrils above water.

WALLET STUFF CAN BE SOME OF THE MOST QUANTIFIABLE AND OBVIOUSLY OPPRESSIVE STUFF IN OUR LIVES. And that's good news, because spotting it is the first step toward becoming free from it. But that doesn't mean it isn't going to hurt. Some of the symptoms of wallet stuff can be ugly when viewed in the bright light of day, but we can't let our feelings of disgust dissuade us from a richer and more satisfying life.

1: Never Enough Stuff

> "Not he who has little, but he who wishes for more, is poor."
> —SENECA

Webster's dictionary defines **envy** as *"a painful or resentful awareness of an advantage enjoyed by another joined with a desire to possess the same advantage."* Have you ever been painfully aware of the advantage of someone around you? Have you ever wanted what they had? Have you ever said to yourself, *I just want_____—is that so much to ask?* Envy is a cruel emotion that entices us to compare ourselves with others and, in doing so, to decide that somehow our lot is second-rate. Envy is also a liar—it tells us that whatever we don't have is better than what we do have. But the trick is as soon as we have it, it's no longer enviable and therefore no longer as desirable. So envy is never satisfied; it only grows the more it's fed.

No one is immune to the temptation of envy. **It's human to want more than you have**—especially when you see someone else with what you don't have. You see envy even in small children, who scream, "That's no fair!" when they see another kid getting more than they got.

Envy isn't a new thing either. Jesus spoke about it in the parable of the day laborers (Matthew 20:1-16), when those who worked the whole day screamed about getting paid the same as the guys who had only worked one hour. "Not fair!" they said. "We want to work less and get paid the same, or if we work more, we should get paid for it."

But *ENVY ISN'T SO MUCH ABOUT ACCUSING THE PERSON WITH MORE BUT ABOUT POINTING THE FINGER AT GOD, WHO GAVE IT TO THEM.* Whether we are conscious of it or not, any time we envy what someone else has, we are like the day laborer, calling God an unfair employer. If we embrace the reality of a God who is all-powerful (Luke 1:37), who determines our steps (Proverbs 16:9), and who gives all good and perfect gifts (James 1:17), then we have to accept that he is the one responsible for our lot and the lot of the Joneses. And there are a few things we have to ask ourselves here: Do we really believe that God desires good things for us? Would we want any more than what God considers best for us? Can't we be content with God's best?

Tweet ♪

Envy leads to more stuff. Volunteer at a homeless shelter to help others and kill envy at the same time. #Unstuff

When we envy other people, our stuffing goes up and our sense of contentment goes down. **The problem with our fascination**

with stuff is that we never get enough (Ecclesiastes 1:8). But when we take our eyes off our lack and put them on God's fullness, envy fades away. When we start to thank God for what he has given as well as what he has not given, envy becomes a thing of the past. We have to ask ourselves, Is stuff really what makes us happy? Or is there something more? Do we need more stuff . . . or more of him who created it?

2: Can't Pay the Bills

> "The only reason a great many American families don't own an elephant is that they have never been offered an elephant for a dollar down and easy weekly payments."
> —MAD MAGAZINE

Did you know that, according to bankrate.com, 72 percent of Americans think that debt is just a part of life, next to impossible to avoid? This mind-set is reflected by the fact that **the total consumer debt in the United States is almost $2.5 trillion**. Based on the latest census statistics, that works out to be nearly $8,100 in debt for every man, woman, and child in the nation.[2] Our debt load is a direct result of our love affair with stuff. Debt is amassed when we want more than we can afford, when we spend more than we make, when we think we "need" what we can't pay for. The modern notion that if we can't afford it, just charge it has been one of the grossest lies of the past century. Credit enslaves borrowers through momentary envy, greed, and self-worship (Proverbs 22:7). It promises a quick fix to our wants and our sufferings, and in a sense it offers us a false way around God's providence. It claims to give us control of our destiny when in reality we should be surrendering that to God.

Debt always gets in the way between us and God. **Debt makes us slaves to the amount we owe and the people we owe it to.** It can lead to stress, worry, lies, cheating, stealing, arguments, and overwork. When we take on debt, we're saying we want more than what God has allotted for us, and we go against his command to "owe nothing to anyone" (Romans 13:8).

Of course there may be times when we are destitute and in dire need of assistance from others in the faith community. And we can't get down on ourselves if borrowing is the only way we can keep food in our stomachs. God's Word even commands us to lend to people who are in need: "Give to those who ask, and don't turn away from those who want to borrow" (Matthew 5:42). Lending isn't a sin; it can be a gift. That means borrowing, in certain situations, is okay too. But that doesn't give us carte blanche to borrow whenever the need (or want) arises. The Bible also tells us to turn the other cheek when someone slaps us (Matthew 5:39), but that doesn't give the slapper the green light to keep on slapping. *IN THE BIBLE, LENDING IS ENCOURAGED FOR THE BENEFIT OF THE GIVER*, who gives to supply a need and to honor God, not for the sake of the borrower. We will never gain more of what we need by accumulating debt.

DEBT LOAD INVENTORY

Do you carry credit card balances month-to-month, year-to-year?
Do you ever find yourself saying things like, "I'll just pay it off at the end of the month"?
When you're considering a purchase, do you worry that if you don't get it now it will be gone?
Do you rationalize a large impulse buy by saying, "I can afford the payments"?

When we make excuses for our purchases, we betray our addiction to stuff. Stuff may make us feel good for a time, but we will still receive the bill. And then the stuff doesn't look so good. How many of us have credit card debt that is so old we've already used up, broken, or thrown away the stuff we're still trying to pay off? Debt is like worry: it gives you something to do (or buy), but it doesn't get you anywhere but off track.

Tweet

> Refuse to "get 10% off today" by opening a new credit card. Credit just makes it easier to buy more than you need or can afford. #Unstuff

3: Overworked

> "As soon as you begin to live the life of faith in God, fascinating and luxurious prospects will open up before you, and these things are yours by right; but if you are living the life of faith you will exercise your right to waive your rights, and let God choose for you." —OSWALD CHAMBERS

If you're feeling overworked, there's a good chance it's a sign of stuffing. The constant need for more keeps us in chains to our income. The more stuff we accumulate, the more bills there are to be paid and the more we have to work. The first thing to ask yourself to diagnose this problem is if your work comes between you and God. There is nothing inherently wrong with working hard—work is a gift from God, and it shouldn't be avoided. But even God's gifts can become a curse, and if hard work leads to sin, it has gone from gift to god.

The sin of overwork is seen in things like worry,

fear, anger, bitterness, lack of time for God, lack of time for family, and lack of time for rest. The big problem with being overworked is that it has the tendency to force us to put a job at the top of the list. Since the top of the list should be reserved for God alone, that makes work a little god.

When someone is a slave, that person is forced to work with no choice in the matter. When we become enslaved to our work, *WE ARE ESSENTIALLY GIVING CONTROL TO THAT WORK, MAKING IT OUR MASTER AND OUR GOD.* If our lives are too full of work to be devoted to God, how can we expect to find true joy? If you are feeling overworked, it's time to ask yourself why. In some cases, people have to work long hours at multiple jobs to provide for their families. But more often overwork comes as a result of believing a lie about life on this earth. Do you think work will provide you with recognition, power, or the means to acquire what will make you happy? What lie have you believed about your powerlessness to change your lot in life?

Men are particularly susceptible to being overworked, largely because of their provision muscle. **Men are wired to provide**—it makes them tick—and if the women they provide for require more stuff, men are driven to do whatever they can to make that possible. But no woman does her faith or her man a service by wanting more stuff. And no man does his God or his wife a service by believing that more stuff is what God wants him to provide.

IS WORK A PROBLEM FOR YOU?

If someone looked at your daily routine, would they say you have more reliance on yourself or on God?

In everything, if we let our work be for God rather than our own accumulation, our lives and work will bring joy rather than strain and fatigue.

4: Stressed

Stress is an unavoidable part of adulthood . . . right? Stress typically comes when we are experiencing a situation where more is required of us than we think we can give, and most of us just assume that's the way life is. We stress when we have a project due that seems undoable, when we have a bill to pay that seems unpayable, when we have a lifestyle to sustain that seems unsustainable. When we stress, we let a certain thing or situation—a stressor—become more powerful and controlling than our devotion to God. Stress can be a sin on several levels. For one thing, it silently destroys God's temple, your body (1 Corinthians 6:19-20). And giving in to stress essentially means you're calling God a liar (Matthew 6:25-32; Philippians 4:6-7). ***Stress results from our assumption that God isn't enough so we have to take up the slack.*** Stress focuses on the need for salvation instead of on the Savior. It is the result of a life that hasn't focused itself on things above but on things within.

Maybe it seems surprising that there's any correlation between stuff and stress. But **stress is actually a symptom of stuffing**. The more we give in to our desire for stuff, the more we have to do to maintain the high stuff gives us. It's like feeding a bad habit: the more we do the thing, the more it demands from us. And the more stuff we own, the more time and effort it requires of us. The car payments have to be made, the security alarm needs to be

Michael

When we got married, one of our favorite new rituals was going grocery shopping together. But soon I noticed a slightly disturbing pattern in Hayley: every time we went to the store, she would buy a couple of cans of green beans. "Don't we already have green beans?" I would ask. Hayley would respond, "I'm not sure, but I want to be safe." Even when we got home and there were six cans of green beans ready to greet the two newest members of our cupboard family, Hayley defended herself. "It's not that many!" When I pointed out that we lived one mile from the store and I could always get more if we ran out, we discovered a little pattern of stuff that was causing stress in Hayley's life. It came from the fear of not having enough for a rainy day. The fear of disaster (Proverbs 3:25-26) was the root of Hayley's stressful shopping practices.

monitored, the computer needs to be fixed. And so it goes that the more stuff we accumulate, the more of us it demands.

The continual monitoring, cleaning, protecting, storing, straightening, and upgrading of stuff leads to all kinds of stress-induced emotional ills. Some of these include anxiety, anger, depression, irritability, frustration, and overreaction to problems.

> "You need not be afraid of sudden disaster or the destruction that comes upon the wicked, for the LORD is your security. He will keep your foot from being caught in a trap." PROVERBS 3:25-26

The truth is that ***TOO MUCH STUFF CAN LEAD TO TOO MUCH STRESS***. But thankfully, stress is avoidable. Stress might confront us, but it is possible to respond to it, like all temptation, with truth. When we start believing that we can live on less, not more, we can be set free from the pressures and stresses that keep us slaves to managing all our stuff.

TweeT ♪

Stress surrounds stuff. ID one thing that stresses you out and see if you can limit it, cancel it, or give it away. #Unstuff

5: Too Much Junk

Owning so much that it goes to waste is another symptom of stuffing. The more we bring into our lives, the more we tend to waste. When stuff is rare, we hold it in high regard. But when it bloats us and overfills us, it simply isn't very valuable anymore. An impoverished child would never have to be told to eat what's on the plate or be punished for giving part of a meal to the dog. We waste when we have an overabundance.

Life on the Road, Day 24

Hayley: How much do we require to live? I used to think I needed much more than I do now. There was a time I thought I required certain stuff to live—stuff that was really luxury, now that I look at it. Today we talked to several women living on the streets in Denver. And it hit me: has my luxury contributed to their poverty? Why would I spend money on entertainment or extravagance when that same money could clothe or even shelter another human being? My soul feels ugly to me today.

So is waste such a bad thing? Some would say it's just the normal result of having plenty. But a more biblical approach would take exception to that philosophy. ***Our abundance was never meant to be wasted or thrown in the garbage heap, but to be used wisely.*** Think about the parable of the three servants with the bags of silver (Matthew 25:14-30). The master left three men with money he wanted a return on. He didn't want them to waste what they had been given but to invest it and make more. Two of the servants doubled their money with their investments, but the third simply sat on the money and gained nothing in return.

Now consider your abundance, however small or great it may be. Could you do something to make it grow? Could it be worth more to the Kingdom going to someone else, or is waste really the best option? To put it in more practical terms, if we have twenty pairs of shoes in our closets, how many of those go to waste? And are there other people who could benefit from a new pair of shoes? Or if we have extra food, how much of it could we share with those who need it more than we do? Jesus put it like this: "To those who use well what they are given, even more will be given, and they will have an abundance. But from those who do nothing, even what little they have will be taken away" (Matthew 25:29). His admonishment is to use well what we have been given. **A thing wasted is not a thing used well.**

WAYS TO TELL IF YOU HAVE TOO MUCH JUNK

Do you find rotten fruit and vegetables stuffed in the back of the fridge?

Do the boxes on your pantry shelves expire before you eat them?

Do you have clothes in your closet you haven't worn in years?

Is your garage stashed with odds and ends that you'll probably never use?

If you survey your life and see large areas of waste, then something has to be done. Waste fails to see the value of the gifts of God and instead treats them like a spoiled child's toys, mishandled and taken for granted.

> A rich man wanted 2 follow Jesus. Jesus said, "Sell it all," but the man didn't. R there things u couldn't part with for Christ? #Unstuff

6: Shopping as Therapy

"I always say shopping is cheaper than a psychiatrist."
—Tammy Faye Bakker

RETAIL THERAPY, ALSO KNOWN AS SHOPPING, IS ABOUT LOOKING FOR COMFORT AND MEDICATION THROUGH THE PURCHASE OF GOODS AND SERVICES. Okay, time for a little self-reflection: do you get some relief or even a sort of high from making a purchase? Though stuff can bring pleasure, it was never meant to be our healer, comforter, or provider. When we look to stuff or the purchase of stuff to meet our emotional needs, we sure aren't looking to God to be our healer and provider. In effect, then, stuff replaces God—if only for a moment—and then all hell breaks loose.

Shopping therapy isn't really therapy at all—it only numbs or hides the problem. It gives the shopper another fix, which might feel like healing temporarily, although it's anything but. Shopping drives the stuff addict deeper into the habit. There is a certain release that comes to the purchaser's heart when she walks through her favorite store picking up items that will soon be hers. Just as runners' bodies become filled with endorphins as they race down the street, so the shopper's body experiences a high as she races through the racks. It's magical. The smells, the sights, and the ecstasy of buying something new presses us to buy more, shop more, want more. Unfortunately, the high we come home with never lasts for long. Soon the stuff gets old and we want new stuff.

Maybe you aren't a traditional shopping addict, and you think you're off the hook. But ***even super frugal buyers can have their own style of retail therapy***. You might clip coupons, get amazing deals, and never pay full price. Maybe you can relate to comedian Rita Rudner, who said, "Buying something on sale is a very special feeling. In fact, the less I pay for something, the more it is worth to me. I have a dress that I paid so little for that I am afraid to wear it. I could spill something on it, and then how would I replace it for that amount of money?" The feeling you get from a great deal can be just as powerful as the feeling the shopaholic gets from paying full price. While purchasing wisely is a good thing, when it becomes an obsession, it's a red flag.

Shopping therapy might soothe your nerves for a moment, but the net result is just more stress, debt, and strife. If shopping therapy is your remedy of choice for those hard and trying days, then it's time to kill the part of you that relies too heavily on stuff. It's time to Unstuff. Oswald Chambers said it well: **"Never nourish an experience which has not God as its Source, and faith in God as its result. If you do, your experience is anti-Christian, no matter what visions you may have had."**

"God is our merciful Father and the source of all comfort."
2 CORINTHIANS 1:3

Tweet♪

Want to break your habit of shopping as therapy? Go to the mall, sit on a bench in front of your fav store, and pray for ppl u see. #Unstuff

7: Highfalutinism

"Where riches hold the dominion of the heart, God has lost His authority." —JOHN CALVIN

This section is one that's going to make a lot of people mad. *LUX-URY*—or highfalutinism, as we call it—**can often be a symptom of too much stuffing**. The truth is that very little stuff is required for life. Human life can be sustained with a few basic elements: adequate food, water, and shelter. Anything above that should be considered a luxury, and though luxury isn't a sin, our notion that luxury is a requirement for happiness is. There is no requirement for happiness other than the will to be happy. This is evidenced in the

WARNING SIGNS YOU MIGHT BE SUFFERING FROM HIGHFALUTINISM

Do you think comfort is a necessity?
Do you travel first-class?
Do you eat at all the best places?
Do you always have the latest technological gadget?
Are you a clothes-label snob?
Does your coffee have to come with a brand name
(like Fourbucks)?

command in James 1:2: "When troubles come your way, consider it an opportunity for great joy."

While he walked this earth, Jesus owned little—in fact, he was more often than not homeless and penniless. This homeless man was very fond of telling people that they needed to die to themselves and turn their lives over to him. His life was far from a life of luxury, so what does that mean for us? Is luxury unbiblical? Perhaps not, but it is crucial for each of us to ask ourselves how we look at stuff, especially luxuries. ***One of the ways we continue to die to self, as Christ commands (Matthew 10:38-39), is by dying to our need to please ourselves.*** Self-pleasing was never Jesus' aim, and should never be the aim of his followers, either (Luke 9:23). But how many of us expend inordinate amounts of energy trying to fill our own happiness tanks? And what is luxury if not an attempt to self-please?

If luxury is our obsession, if it is the predominant characteristic of our lives, then we need to consider whether stuff has jumped into the front seat, ahead of even the God we say we serve.

On the pages of Scripture, Jesus is recorded only a few times as asking people to give up everything they owned: the rich man (Luke 18:18-25) and his own disciples (Luke 9:3, 57-62; 14:33). He may or may not be asking you to do the same, but he is certainly asking each of us to meet the needs of others. And **where the pursuit of luxury impedes our ability to give, we have a problem**. In the Bible we are given this bit of direction: "Give in proportion to what you have. Whatever you give is acceptable if you give it eagerly. And give according to what you have, not what you don't have. Of course, I don't mean your giving should make life easy for others and hard for yourselves. I only mean that there should be some equality" (2 Corinthians 8:11-13). Equality. Wow, that sounds radical. But at the heart of it is the spirit of love. If we have enough to indulge ourselves with luxury, don't we have enough to share with those in need? That's the Christian spirit—one that thinks more highly of others and considers their needs as important as our own, if not more important.

Tweet ♪

Are nice things a "need" for u? Take 1 expensive item and give it away, then find a replacement at a thrift store. #Unstuff

"Be humble, thinking of others as better than yourselves. Don't look out only for your own interests, but take an interest in others, too. You must have the same attitude that Christ Jesus had. Though he was God, he did not think of equality with God as something to cling to. Instead, he gave up his divine privileges; he took the humble position of a slave and was born as a human being. When he appeared in human form, he humbled himself in obedience to God and died a criminal's death on a cross." PHILIPPIANS 2:3-8

If we are being honest with ourselves about our faith, we have to take a long, hard look at the luxury in our lives compared to the lack in the lives of others. After all, Christ is our model. What more can you do to die to self, to serve the greater need, and to humble yourself like your Savior? Whatever you do, *DON'T LET IT BE SAID OF YOU* when you die **that "you have spent your years on earth in luxury, satisfying your every desire**. You have fattened yourselves for the day of slaughter" (James 5:5). Consider the opportunity to Unstuff your life for the sake of others your true luxury.

"One of the ways of manifesting and maintaining the crucifixion of the flesh is never to use money to gratify it." —ANDREW MURRAY

Life on the Road, Day 26

Michael: We're in Denver, Colorado. Work is going well, and we decided to treat ourselves to a nice dinner as a change from mac and cheese. The food was amazing, but something wasn't quite right the whole dinner. I couldn't fully enjoy it, and I didn't know why. Then the bill came. Almost a hundred and twenty bucks. I looked up at Hayley and said, "We just ate twenty-four Subway footlong sandwiches." She instantly tracked with me and said, "Things are never going to be the same for us."

8: A Cluttered Life

The average North American consumes ten times as much as the average person living in China and thirty times as much as the average person living in India.

It doesn't take a lot of money or finery to have too much. The production of stuff is the primary function of most of the world. We could have a house full of stuff without even giving it much effort. In fact, just bring in the mail every day and see how long it takes to have a house full of stuff. Did you know that the U.S. Postal Service delivers more than 100 billion pieces of junk mail every year?[3]

We have a friend whose grandma has a problem with stuff. She collects it, all of it. Her house is nothing but a maze of junk that you have to squeeze through in order to enter. Magazines, newspapers, and junk mail piled up as high as your shoulders line the halls and fill the rooms. *Her obsession with stuff won't allow her*

Michael

My dad kept the family garage in a condition of perpetual clutter. It was overrun by rarely used tools, broken furniture, and even an old freezer that was full of roadkill he collected for future use in hand-tying flies and lures for fly-fishing. He'd spin their fur and feathers around hooks to make his own "flies." Clutter isn't a good feeling for anybody (especially a kid who just went to the freezer for a popsicle).

to throw any of it away. Maybe she thinks she might need it someday or that it has some future value. Whatever her motivation, now the stuff consumes her rather than her consuming the stuff.

Humans are messy by nature. We have a hard time keeping things in their place, but that doesn't mean we like the mess. We want it all put away neatly, but life doesn't always turn out like we want it to. The truth is that **if we had less stuff, we'd have less mess**. So we need to Unstuff.

CLUTTER CAN BE A SILENT, DESTRUCTIVE FORCE. It doesn't make a sound, but every time we see it, it causes a little more stress. The mess around us can bring us down and make us sluggish, lazy, and even depressed. A lot of people find it hard to think when things are a mess—they feel the need to straighten things up, or they might

---

ANALYZING YOUR CLUTTER

Open up your closet and find an item in the back. When is the
    last time you used it? In the past week? month? year?
    (If your answer is the last year, it's time to get rid of it.)
Are you afraid to get rid of this item? If so, why?
Does this object seem to offer you some kind of better future
    or present? Will it deliver on this promise?

---

just feel the oppression of stuff weighing them down. Clutter isn't good for us or for our giving muscle either. In collecting clutter, what we're really doing is hoarding the gifts of God rather than moving them along to someone who could really use them.

Tweet ♪

Tired of clutter? Find 5 things to sell, give, or throw away each day for 1 month. You'll be surprised by how much you don't need! #Unstuff

9: Failure to Give

"What a wonderful religion Christianity is. It takes money, the very embodiment of the power of sense of this world, with its self-interest, its covetousness, and its pride, and it changes it into an instrument for God's service and glory."
—ANDREW MURRAY

The Parable of the Delivery Driver

There once was a delivery driver whose job it was to pick up packages at the warehouse and deliver them to their recipients. Every day he would start up his truck, load it with boxes and envelopes, and drive off . . . home. At home he would pull the truck into the garage, shut the door, and start to unload. Every box and envelope, every package, went onto shelves that lined his huge steel garage. After unloading, he would pick a few packages and take them into his house to open. Then he'd spend the rest of the day going through everyone else's mail to see what interested him. If he liked something, he would keep it, and if not, he'd just throw it into the Dumpster in the backyard. But most of it he kept, because he liked it all. Eventually, though, all the shippers of these items contacted the owner of the delivery company. And when the driver's twisted system of hoarding and theft was discovered, he was summarily fired and hauled off to jail.

This story no doubt sounds far-fetched, but it's not so far off from what we often do with the gifts God gives us. When God gives us something, how do we know it's not meant to be delivered to someone else? God distributes necessities to his people through the hands of other people. Up to now you might not have thought of yourself as a delivery driver, but think about it: how might you deliver for God?

What we're talking about here is an essential but unfortunately reclusive part of the Christian faith known as generosity. If we don't want anything to come between us and God, we need to give this concept some thought. In his letter to Timothy, Paul explains it this way: *"Tell them to use their money to do good. They should be rich in good works and generous to those in need, always being ready to share with others"* (1 Timothy 6:18).

When we were little, sharing was a hard concept for all of us. When another kid took our toys, our first and most basic instinct was to scream with all our might, "Mine!" Our parents were quick to tell us we needed to share, and over time, if only reluctantly, most of us learned to give up what was ours and sit by as another enjoyed it. But have we fully embraced the concept? Or are we still holding back much of our stuff, fearful of watching someone else enjoy it? Is it hard for you to imagine giving half of what is yours away for someone else's use? If so, this next command will give you fits. But check it out: "If you have two shirts, give one to the poor. If you have food, share it with those who are hungry" (Luke 3:11). If you have two, give one away. Wow—that's half of what you own, and it's a hard pill to swallow.

The notion of giving away our money and the things we own is classic Christianity. It was a foundational concept that the early church was built on: "All the believers met together in one place and shared everything they had. They sold their property and possessions and shared the money with those in need" (Acts 2:44-45). This kind of radical obedience proves that as children of God we believe the things of this earth are really of little value compared to the riches we have in heaven.

Radical acts of obedience have a sort of intuitive reciprocity inherent in every act. We can see this concept at work in the area of forgiveness, too: "If you forgive those who sin against you, your heavenly Father will forgive you. But if you refuse to forgive others, your Father will not forgive your sins" (Matthew 6:14-15). We get what we give. And that concept repeats itself in the area of generosity: *"THOSE WHO SHUT THEIR EARS TO THE CRIES OF THE POOR WILL BE IGNORED IN THEIR OWN TIME OF NEED"* (Proverbs 21:13). As a believer, you—and everything you have—belong to God. So what you do or don't do with what you have has great significance for your relationship with him. Not that it's some kind of cosmic karma thing, where you give just so you can get (that would be selfishness, not holiness), but we give so that God might get the glory, knowing full well that he will honor our acts of faith.

When we hear there is an investigation underway to find out if someone in the government overspent or "misallocated funds" in a certain area, is it any real surprise? Why does it seem that money is so easy to spend when it isn't ours? The notion that money can be used without any regard for who it really belongs to is infuriating to the average taxpayer. Yet **how many times do we take the money and gifts God has given us to serve him and others and use them for ourselves?**

Tweet ♪

We are born saying "Mine!" Say "Yours" today in an unexpected way by generously giving something to someone in need. #Unstuff

The world cares about what we own, while God cares about how we use what we own. As believers we can be sure that everything we have—our possessions, our supplies, our time, and our energy—is a gift from God, and it's crucial that we understand the purpose of those gifts. The world around us is obsessed with accumulation, but God is not. After all, Jesus taught that "it is more blessed to give than to receive" (Acts 20:35).

But by our accounting, that paradigm seems completely upside down. **Giving, by its very definition, means having less.** If you have five books and you give away three of them, you are left with only two. So where is the blessing in that? We need a mental shift for this to make sense: blessing is not found in the amount of stuff we surround ourselves with but in the joy we receive from doing the will of God—in the contentment we find in needing less and trusting God with our supply. The blessings of God come to those who find nothing more valuable than doing his will.

some final stuff

1. Charles Spurgeon once said that discernment is not a matter of simply telling the difference between right and wrong; rather, it is telling the difference between right and almost right. What about you—have you gotten your affair with stuff almost right? And are you able to discern the difference between what's good and what's best?

2. Given what you know now, are you willing to take a chance and Unstuff your life? What are some of the things holding you back?

3. What value does stuff have in the world's eyes? What value can your stuff have in God's economy?

4. What is one thing God says about wallet stuff that you need to start putting into action?

MONEY
MONDAY NIGHT
JUNK
CLOSETS
PANEL
SAFETY VACATION
SLEEP SKI
CREDIT
FOOD
STUDY
VIDEO GAMES
JEWELRY
TWITTER

MIND STUFF

Section Two

unstuff.org

We've established by now that TOO MUCH OF A GOOD THING CAN BE TOO MUCH. Our lives, our homes, our cars, and our desks are cluttered with stuff. But our environment isn't the only thing that can become stuffed; our minds can also become so bloated that there's no room for all the good things we need, like peace, joy, hope, contentment, and trust. Just like a room that is cluttered with items that have no assigned place, so our minds can be cluttered with thoughts that have no appropriate place in the mind of a believer. When we let thoughts about stuff constantly fill our minds, the healthy and godly thoughts that would bring order to our chaos get crowded out.

This condition of mind cluttering doesn't happen overnight—it's something that occurs gradually. **As small children, we had no cares at all.** Our lives were lived from one adventure to the next. Every experience was new and filled with an almost fantastical vision of what life might hold. When we imagined the future, it was rarely with dread but instead with eager anticipation. We didn't worry about much other than whether someone was playing with *our* toy. If we were down, it didn't take much to bring us back up again—some cookies and milk, our favorite cartoon, or even just a kiss and a hug. We found joy in the little things—exploring the backyard, making a fort out of a cardboard box, or lying on the grass watching the clouds float by. But the more we became aware of the differences between ourselves and other kids—the more we saw our lack—the more we started to want what other people had and resent what we were "stuck with."

Michael When I was a child, my family was poor—I just didn't know it until high school. My first clue should have been that there were eight of us living in an eight-hundred-square-foot house with one bathroom. There were other signs, too, like the fact that the utilities got turned off from time to time or that no bill got paid until it was delivered in the pink envelope. But I didn't realize anything was different about my life until I was a teenager and started noticing that everyone else had color TVs, microwaves, cable, two cars, and their own bedroom. It is said that it isn't what surrounds us or happens to us that matters but what we think about what happens to us. I didn't become poorer the older I got—I just became more discontented.

Life has a way of testing us and forcing us to choose between truth and a lie, and a lot of the time we happily choose the lie in order to have more of what we want. We mistakenly believe that what the world is dishing out is not only digestible but really good for us. And so we dig in to a mind-set that's informed by the world's standards, and the result is a weak life and an even weaker faith. **The natural order of things is to decay— to go from neat to messy, from life to death.** A room doesn't clean itself, as our mothers have often said, and a mind doesn't clean up its own clutter either. It takes work and a spiritually concerted effort to clean things up mentally and get back to the truth (Philippians 4:8).

In this section you'll find a few telltale signs that your mind has

Michael

If you're like me, you can look at the lines of a beautiful car and melt. The sensation is physical: our mouths start to water, our heart rates increase, our pupils dilate. Our bodies have a visceral reaction to beauty, especially the kind of beauty found in the fine art of cars. And because of that Hayley and I buy cars—often. We sell cars—often.

I enjoy hunting for great deals on cars and passing them on to the next owner. I admit that I have expensive taste, and I would love nothing more than to drive a new Audi A8 or Mercedes S-Class off the lot. Ain't nothin' better than that new-car smell (German cars smell like strudel!). But when we decided to Unstuff our lives, we gave some serious thought to *why* we wanted a brand-new expensive car when an inexpensive used car would serve the same purpose. Most of it came down to image: *I don't want people to think I'm a 1999 Ford Taurus. When they look at me, I want them to see me as a Mercedes S-Class.*

Now some people facing this dilemma might come to the conclusion, "Let's buy the junkiest car we can find and use it as our public testimony about Unstuffing!" And to you I say, "Bravo!" But I took a less extreme route. Cars are one of my hobbies, and I like passing on my good deals to friends when I'm done driving them. So we buy cars that were once $60,000 for $6,000. Sure, they're fifteen years old and have around a hundred thousand miles on them, but Hayley and I take joy in that we didn't pay $54,000 more for the same item that someone else did and that we were able to pay cash for it. For us, Unstuffing wasn't just about the math; we also had to get to the *why* underneath. We had to retrain our minds to tell our wallets that a huge car payment forever was not okay.

been adversely affected by stuff. If you find yourself spending time on any of these kinds of thoughts, consider how that's working for you and how things might be different if you defied the status quo.

10: Obsessed over What Other People Think

The more stuff we own, want, or guard, the more our thoughts become filled with the things of this world. *AND THE MORE OUR THOUGHTS ARE FILLED WITH THE THINGS OF THIS WORLD, THE MORE CONCERNED WE BECOME ABOUT WHAT THE WORLD THINKS.* We enjoy our stuff, sure, but we also enjoy how it makes other people think about us. How many of our life decisions have been made based on how others will view us? In everything from wardrobe choices to our line of work, we are influenced by how we look to those around us.

When we make decisions based not on morality or necessity but on our image, we become silent slaves to the people whose approval we are hoping to gain. To those of us stuck in this trap, Paul offers this striking statement: "If pleasing people were my goal, I would not be Christ's servant" (Galatians 1:10).

Any number of things can send us reeling into approval-seeking mode. The places we live, the schools we send our kids to, the stores we shop at, the churches we attend—all can be significantly influenced by what other people will think of us. It's said that you can please some of the people some of the time, but you can't please all of the people all of the time. Well, it's true, and that's what makes obsessing over what others think of us such a futile and even dangerous proposition. But God has made it clear what pleases him: he is pleased by our devotion and obedience to him (Matthew 7:21; John 14:15).

A funny thing happens when we take our focus off the stressful

WHO ARE YOU TRYING TO IMPRESS?

If you got a new car, who would be impressed?

What's one thing you could do with the car you have that would please God?

If you redecorated your house, who would like you more, and what does that say about them?

Who could you invite into your home this week as a way to please God?

How would you feel if your house was messy when you had people over?

Does a messy house ever keep you from having guests?

If you updated your wardrobe, who would you be hoping to impress?

Where could you donate a bag of clothes as a way to please God?

What would happen if you shopped only at thrift shops for the next year?

and impossible task of pleasing everyone and put it onto pleasing God. Suddenly other people's opinions no longer control us, no longer affect our spirits or our emotions. *We are set free.* The chains that bound us to the world are loosed, and we are able to breathe again. As you Unstuff, we challenge you to think about your desire to impress others. How can you switch your focus from trying to impress earthlings to living humbly for God?

Tweet ♪

Invest the average car payment every month, and you're a millionaire in 27 years. That's some Camry. Pay cash for a clunker! #Unstuff

11: Discontentment

Walking into his friend's house one morning, a rich man heard his friend say, "Oh, if I just had $5,000, I could pay my bills and be at peace!" Feeling in a blessing kind of mood, the rich man went to his car, got his checkbook, and wrote a $5,000 check to his friend. Then he went back inside and handed it to him. His friend was blown away. He couldn't stop thanking him. But the rich man had to go, so he said his good-byes and left. As soon as the rich man was gone, his friend said, "Rats! Why didn't I say $10,000?"

With so many things to focus on in this world, it's a mystery why we so often choose the bad ones. It's true there are lots of things we don't have. We might not have the house we want or the gift of singing we wish we had. We might not be as good at our job as other people are. But when we focus on our lack rather than our plenty, our failures instead of our successes, we're entering the murky waters of discontentment. And in the process, we put ourselves in danger of turning even our successes into failures.

When we focus on what we don't have instead of what we do have, we need to call it what it is: **discontentment**. It's *NOT BEING HAPPY WITH WHAT GOD HAS ALLOWED IN OUR LIVES*. Being discontented is kind of like calling God a bad gifter or a lousy architect for drawing up such terrible blueprints for our lives. In essence, we're saying to God, "You haven't given me enough 'good and perfect'! I want more!" In these instances it is all about *me*. And at the heart of that discontented self-centeredness is pride, the foundation of all sin. Pride fuels the fire of discontentment and a woe-is-me attitude of self-pity. Will we choose to resent the life we've been given and wish for another? Or will we choose the appreciated life . . . which is also the good life?

Before we can engage in a balanced discussion about the other

BREEDING GROUNDS FOR DISCONTENTMENT

Financial discontentment: the state of never being happy with the spending status quo. When people are financially discontented, their desire for stuff supersedes their ability to acquire it. They spend their lives trying to get more money and more stuff to fill the hole of emptiness inside.

Spiritual discontentment: the state of always wanting more spiritual highs. People who are spiritually discontented can't accept the valley. They always want the mountaintop and wonder why God would allow bad things in their lives. So they accumulate more stuff—books, Bible studies, church functions, weekend retreats—in search of that high. While those things are good, they can never replace the best thing: God himself.

Physical and emotional discontentment: the state of people not being happy with their bodies or hearts. They hurt somewhere and look for relief immediately. The quickest "cure" for discontentment that presents itself is often stuffing, whether that comes in the form of shopping therapy, relationships, entertainment, sex, gambling, drugs, medication, or anything else that distracts from or numbs the pain.

end of the spectrum, contentment, we need to agree on a definition. **Is contentment the satisfaction of our needs, or is it the control of our desires?** The world essentially says, "Give me what I want, and I'll be happy." But the self-controlled definition is really a more biblically defendable choice. This view says, "I will be content no matter what I get." Thankfully, we're not on our own here—God has given us heavenly sources to control our desires for more than what we've been given. And those resources are of great value for the believer who has much or little. The apostle Paul learned the secret to contentment: "I have learned how to be content with whatever I have. I know how to live on almost nothing or with everything. I have learned the secret of living in every situation, whether it is with a full stomach or empty, with plenty or little. For I can do everything through Christ, who gives me strength" (Philippians 4:11-13).

What is more important to you: your comfort on earth or your position in heaven? How much you don't have that the rest of the world has or how much you do have that the rest of the world needs? What you have or don't have in this world is irrelevant in God's eyes. He owns all the cattle on a thousand hills (Psalm 50:10), and he can accomplish what needs to be done with or without your stuff. ***If you can find the will to be at peace no matter what God has decided is best for you, you will learn the secret of contentment.*** And it doesn't lie in getting what you want but in wanting what you've got. Do you want what God wants for you? Then want only more of him and his self-sacrificing life in you (Ephesians 4:22-24).

> "True godliness with contentment is itself great wealth." 1 TIMOTHY 6:6

> "So if we have enough food and clothing, let us be content." 1 TIMOTHY 6:8

TweeT ♪

Not content? You don't need more stuff; you need less you and more God. #Unstuff

12: Stuff as Medication

We may have a bunch of rationalizations about why we need our stuff, but a lot of it is simply medication. We get it, buy it, or do

Life on the Road, Day 27

Hayley: This week we got to stay in a hotel for two nights while on business in a big city. It was such luxury to be able to stand up straight in the shower and order room service. It was a fun night for all of us, but the next morning we longed to get back into the motor home—our space, our place, our home. And that's when we knew that our experiment was working.

it in order to get better or to feel better. **Medications, whether they are emotional, spiritual, financial, or physical, are used to dull pain or remove suffering.** But some pain isn't meant to be dulled. And suffering isn't a cockroach to be squashed as quickly as it enters the light. Consider these words in James: "When troubles come your way, consider it an opportunity for great joy. For you know that when your faith is tested, your endurance has a chance to grow. So let it grow, for when your endurance is fully developed, you will be perfect and complete, needing nothing" (James 1:2-4). Rather than letting our suffering draw us closer to him, medication covers it up with toys, sensations, and distractions.

THE BIBLICAL PRESCRIPTION FOR SUFFERING IS ENDURANCE, NOT MEDICATION. You don't endure poverty by striving to buy more. You don't endure grief by running to the arms of the next person who you think will complete you. And you don't grow in faith when you run from the truth of your spiritual poverty and try to rack up more credits on your "report card" for your small group. Bible studies, small groups, and relationships aren't evil in themselves, but they become destructive when they are used as a "get out of testing free" card—an ointment for our pain, a way out of the testing. Consider what Jesus did when he was faced with the incomprehensible pain of the Cross (Luke 22:39-43). He didn't avoid the pain or self-medicate; his choice was "I want your will to be done, not mine." Jesus chose suffering so that we would be saved. His discomfort and agony were required for our salvation, and no medication would have done what his blood did for us.

SELF-MEDICATION INVENTORY

When you're feeling down, what is your medication of choice? Comfort foods? Mindless TV? Shopping? Sleep? Going online?

What tangible steps can you take to replace those self-medication habits with something more productive and godly?

Who is going to keep you accountable in your journey toward Unstuffing your self-medication?

It could quite possibly be one of the biggest goals of the evil one to convince God's people that suffering is our enemy. But suffering can be our friend when it isn't at our own hands. (Just read the book of Job or the story of Joseph in Genesis for a couple of examples.)

Tweet

> Addiction is medicating with stuff instead of letting God fill that place in your life. Admit you have a prob and make a plan to #Unstuff.

13: Instant Gratification

If cooking a meal takes more than ten minutes, we don't want to fix it. When we hear a song we love on satellite radio, we have the app that tags it and lets us download it immediately onto our iPod. When we sit down to a good meal, we eat the whole plateful instead of saving half of it for tomorrow. **We want instant gratification, and we want it now.**

Back in the day, we had to use something called dial-up to get on the Internet. It dialed up using your phone line, and the connection took forever to make, all while making a terrible sound: *WEEEEEEORRRRRRRRWAAAAAAAAAH!* Now we have silent, lightning-fast, wireless routers and instant online access almost everywhere we go. If we have to wait more than three seconds for a Web site to load, we just Google another one. *If anything takes too much time, we just aren't interested.*

Because stuff is so quick to come by these days, we have become more ravenous and more stuff-crazy. But have you ever stopped to consider what impact instant gratification has on your relationship with God?

At a very basic level, **stuff interrupts our pursuit of patience**. When our cravings are gratified instantly, we never have the opportunity to exercise that part of our spirits. Patience is considered a spiritual benefit because it teaches us to rely on God, to disregard our flesh with all its desires, and to trust that God will work everything out for good (Romans 5:4; Hebrews 10:36; James 1:4).

> "We can rejoice, too, when we run into problems and trials, for we know that they help us develop endurance." ROMANS 5:3

Patient endurance is a virtue the world discarded long ago. It carries with it the concepts of *slow*, *silent*, and *long*. And in this wireless and fiber-optic era, who wants any of those traits to be a part of their lives? *No, WE WANT THINGS TO HAPPEN NOW—IF NOT SOONER.*

Instant gratification isn't inherently bad. It's human nature to want to eat quickly or to find the answers you need at the touch of a button. But when instant gratification keeps us focused on the stuff we want next rather than the stuff God wants to teach us, it is getting in the way of our relationship with God. Our preoccupation with desiring the pleasures of this life keeps us from spiritual maturity and hinders us from the peace, hope, and joy that we assume instant gratification would bring us. Ironically it's not getting what we want instantly that leads to spiritual maturity. **It is patience and endurance, not instant gratification, that makes us "perfect and complete, needing nothing"** (James 1:4).

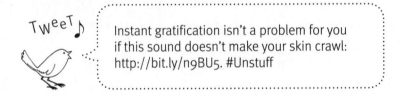

Tweet ♪

Instant gratification isn't a problem for you if this sound doesn't make your skin crawl: http://bit.ly/n9BU5. #Unstuff

14: Thinking We Deserve More

Another problem with desiring too much stuff is that it can get us thinking that we deserve more than others—that God loves us more than the next guy. We figure we're good people—we don't hurt anyone, we take care of our families and friends and churches— so if anyone deserves more, it's us. It's easy to look around at the evil people of this world, some with wealth and fame, and say, *"I deserve more than they do because they're bad and I'm good."* When we see people succeed and we feel like we should be in their shoes instead, we can become bitter and resentful, envying others and their cool stuff. And that can have a dizzying effect on our fairness bone (connected to the "I've got rights" bone). The more we focus on stuff, the more unfair we think it is when we don't get what others have. And the more we want what we can't have, the more we feel we deserve it. It's a vicious cycle.

It's hard to be thankful when we are so caught up in thinking we deserve more than we have. But there will always be those who have more than we do—and those who have less than we do. We are commanded in Scripture not to complain (Philippians 2:14-15), and we are told that thankfulness is God's will for Christians (1 Thessalonians 5:18). So in the life of faith, there is no room for a mind that thinks it deserves more.

> "Be thankful in all circumstances, for this is God's will for you who belong to Christ Jesus." 1 THESSALONIANS 5:18

As long as we're humans, humility is going to be hard. It feels painful and unnatural to us. But if we're honest and want to talk about what we *really* deserve, we should take a look at the condition of our sinful hearts. In that light, we become keenly aware that we deserve nothing but a life in hell. We deserve nothing of the reward we get as a result of Christ's sacrifice. Yet God, in all his graciousness, allowed us to be saved, even though we had done nothing to deserve it (Ephesians 2:4-5). So who are we, knowing how sinful we are, to believe that we deserve more good things than others? *TRUE HUMILITY—THE KIND THAT ENDURES ALL INJURY AND INJUSTICE WITHOUT RESENTMENT—SAYS, "JUST WHAT GOD HAS GIVEN, NO MORE AND NO LESS."* And it imitates Christ, who didn't consider the injustice done to him anything to resent or complain about (Philippians 2:6-8; 1 Peter 2:22-24). Our lives become more aligned with God and more spiritually successful when we stop assuming we deserve more than others and start thinking they probably deserve more than we do (Philippians 2:3-4).

As long as we believe that our suffering has more to do with injustice than discipline, we will continue to suffer. But we don't have to continue resenting others or seeing our cup as half empty. All it takes is a shift in attitude. When we think more soberly about ourselves and are more honest about our sinfulness and our need for salvation, we can be set free from the chains of ingratitude.

TweeT ♪

If ur a cup-1/2-empty person, end it today by offering someone a drink from ur cup. You'll actually feel better with 1/4 cup. #Unstuff

Life on the Road, Day 40

Michael: There is a good amount of labor that goes into setting up camp: balancing the motor home, hooking up water and sewer, unhooking our tow vehicle. It takes a lot of energy and time, but once it's done, so is my labor. No yard to mow, no gutters to repair, no walls to paint. Living with less means less to fix, and I'm digging that. Check that—I'm gonna go fix that cupboard that flies open going around left-hand turns.

15: Worry

Worry is mind clutter. When we worry, we fill our minds with lies rather than the truth. We mistakenly believe that God won't come through as promised, that the thing we are facing is too big for us. And rather than believing nothing is too big for him, we cram our minds with fears about the future. **Worry rejects God as provider and comforter** and instead encourages us to rely on ourselves to get out of the mess we're in.

Worry seems to be one of those acceptable sins that we have just learned to live with. We consider it too hard to be free from, too difficult to resist. But Jesus has some rather revolutionary things to say about worry. He tells us to forget about the future and focus on the present. When we focus on fear of what might or might not happen, we are choosing to live in fear instead of in God's grace. God operates not in an atmosphere of fear but of belief. His will is for us to live for today and not worry about tomorrow. In Jesus' own words, "Don't worry about tomorrow, for tomorrow will bring its own worries. Today's trouble is enough for today" (Matthew 6:34).

When we fear the future, we are accusing God of not being in control and of not being good. As God's children, willing to do whatever he wills for us, we shouldn't have unknowns about tomorrow because we believe that whatever he desires for us will happen and that his plan will be the best thing for us.

If we truly trust God and his Word, we have no need for fear, and our minds will be uncluttered by the things of this world.

Tweet ♪

Is life stuffed with worry about the future? Accept that God is ur provider and read Matt. 6:34 today: http://ref.ly/Mt6.34;NLT. #Unstuff

---

WORRY INVENTORY

Write down the top five things you tend to worry about. Then
    write down five characteristics you know to be true about God.
Why might God be allowing these sources of worry in your life?
What does God say your response to concerns should be?
Is God big enough to handle what's going on in your life?

16: Feeling Depressed

It's normal for everyone to experience highs and lows throughout
the course of life. But do you feel like you're in a funk more often
than you'd like? There are a number of forms these negative emotions can take—everything from a mild case of feeling down to
being so dark it's necessary to seek medical help. We're not medical professionals, and we recognize that there are often physiological aspects to depression. But we also believe that a lot of times
our thoughts about stuff can lead to cases of the blues or even
depression. Since stuff is mostly neutral, it generally isn't the stuff
itself that depresses us but what we *think* about stuff that makes
us sick. *WHEN WE LET STUFF TAKE A MORE PROMINENT POSITION
THAN GOD, IT CAN LEAD US DOWN A PATH OF DEJECTION AND
HOPELESSNESS.* Instead of focusing on God's faithfulness, we get
hung up in a cycle of resentment, fear, worry, and stress over what
we lack. When we're stuck in this mentality, we forget that God has
already given us everything we need: "By his divine power, God has
given us everything we need for living a godly life" (2 Peter 1:3). A
godly life is a joyful life, not a depressed life. If our world is cen-
tered on stuff—if our focus is the things or people around us more
than the God above us—we are creating a pattern for mental and
emotional idolatry.

When stuff takes a backseat to God, our emotions are

still part of our lives, but they don't control us. Letting go of our attachment to stuff—and even denying stuff to ourselves on occasion—gives us an opportunity to take control of our emotional lives rather than letting them take control of us. Without this kind of self-control, we are bent on becoming victims of our environment rather than victors.

If there was ever a person who had an opportunity for depression, it was Corrie ten Boom. Living under the control of the Nazis in the Ravensbrück concentration camp, Corrie and her sister, Betsie, faced horrific living conditions, including torture and near starvation. But even though her sister eventually died in that awful place, Corrie refused to let it own her soul. *She refused depression and instead took hold of God's Word*, leading worship each night in her bunk. Her environment was a perfect recipe for depression: lack, pain, violence, and neglect. But even in the midst of those agonizing circumstances, she trusted and relied on God.

More than likely, we will never have to experience the total horror Corrie experienced, but there's no question we will be assaulted by varying levels of lack. Depression doesn't offer itself only to people in concentration camps but to all who believe its whispers: "Life isn't fair—you deserve more than this. How can you be expected to go on under such conditions?" But the

---

SPIRITUAL INVENTORY

What beliefs (conscious or unconscious) are weighing you down? Write down five things you believe about your life that make you sad or worried.

How does God's Word line up with those beliefs?

When you're up against difficult circumstances in your life, do you really believe that God is in control (Romans 8:28)?

---

beginning pangs of depression can be rejected and replaced with truth. It all comes down to our faith in God and his ability to protect and lead us. If we don't know the true character of God—if we don't trust him to do what he says—we will become victims of our surroundings.

TweeT ♪

The earth w/o depressions would be flat. #Unstuff your expectation of a flat life— embrace the valleys, and look to the mountains.

17: Emotional Drama

We have a four-year-old who suffers most of her emotional drama at the hands of stuff: the stuff she wants but doesn't get, the stuff we take away from her because she's been disobedient, the stuff she has to share but doesn't want to. We smile about a preschooler's stuff drama when she wails over having dropped half her ice cream on the ground or having to turn off a game she has been playing on the computer, but the truth is that adults aren't all that different.

Hayley

The other day I was unloading groceries from the SUV we'd just gotten two days ago (another of Michael's amazing cash deals). The rear liftgate on the car was up, and so was the garage door. As I came back from the kitchen, I saw my mother pushing the button on the garage door, and almost in slow motion, it started closing. Before I could do anything, there was a horrifying screech as it scraped against the liftgate. I screamed, "Noooo!" as I ran for the door, all the while knowing it was too late. I was beside myself. The garage door had scraped off a streak of paint from the back of the SUV. Talk about emotional drama. Fortunately Michael had a calmer approach when he examined the situation. "That's why we buy used cars with scratches already on them, honey—so we don't have to stress about this kind of stuff. Let me show you a half dozen dings and imperfections you haven't even noticed yet about your 'new' truck." We're learning an important lesson as we Unstuff: *WHEN STUFF ISN'T SO IMPORTANT, IT ISN'T SO EMOTIONALLY CHARGED.*

How many times has the average parent had a meltdown because a beloved item gets broken or ruined by rambunctious kids? It's sad but true: the stuff in our lives is often more valuable to us than the emotional well-being of our family. **It's only when we put stuff in its rightful place that the drama stops.** Stuff should never be an excuse for sin. Emotional drama isn't limited only to the stuff we have, either. It can also come from our lack of stuff. Feelings of resentment, bitterness, and envy are all a result of our feelings about the stuff we wish we had. Interestingly, if you take a look at the Ten Commandments, you'll notice that half of them are about stuff:

1. *Have no other gods (i.e., don't put stuff before God)*
2. *Have no idols (i.e., don't make stuff to worship)*
7. *Do not commit adultery (i.e., don't enjoy what isn't yours)*
8. *Do not steal (i.e., don't take stuff that isn't yours)*
10. *Do not covet (i.e., don't desire someone else's stuff)*

All emotional drama has one source: stuff other than God. **When we love stuff, it sucks us in and demands our devotion.** Sure, you might think you can love stuff and not become its slave, but it never works out that way. The only way to cut out the unnecessary drama in your life is to Unstuff.

Stuff should never be an excuse for sin.

Tweet ♪

> Ugh, drama. #Unstuff ur life by being calm in the midst of crisis today. Nothing ur going through can compare to God on a cross.

18: Being Okay with Acceptable Sins

> "We can readily identify sin in the immoral or unethical conduct of people in society at large. But we often fail to see it in what I call the 'acceptable sins of the saints.' In effect, we, like society at large, live in denial of our sin."
> —JERRY BRIDGES

As modern Christians, we've made some adjustments to our interpretation of sin in our lives. We've looked at the world around us and accepted its standard for what behavior is "normal" and therefore unavoidable. (And besides, we're covered by grace, right?) We might make a distinction for certain "big" sins, but things like worry, fear, lack of self-control, bitterness, resentment, gossip, complaining, anxiety, discontentment, impatience, selfishness, ingratitude, jealousy, judgmentalism, anger, sarcasm, and unkindness are prominent, if not acceptable, in the church community. We might rationalize these sins by saying things like,

"No one's perfect," or, "That's just how I am," or, "I'm just keepin' it real."

But that's not what God intended. *THE BLOOD OF CHRIST IS MEANT TO SAVE US NOT JUST FOR ETERNITY BUT ALSO FROM OUR SIN NOW* (Romans 6:18; 1 Peter 2:24). Just because we have Christ as our Savior doesn't excuse us from the responsibility to recognize sin in our lives and make a concerted effort to get rid of it. In fact, the Bible spells out a zero-tolerance policy for sin when it says, "If we deliberately continue sinning after we have received knowledge of the truth, there is no longer any sacrifice that will cover these sins. There is only the terrible expectation of God's judgment and the raging fire that will consume his enemies" (Hebrews 10:26-27).

Of course there is a remedy for such separation, and it is forgiveness. But forgiveness has a requirement on the life of the forgiven: it calls for confession and repentance, not acceptance (Acts 3:19; 1 John 1:9-10). When we refuse to turn away from the sin in our lives, **this "acceptable" stuff blocks or shipwrecks our spiritual maturity and success as followers of Christ** (1 Timothy 1:19).

If you're like us, then you have a few acceptable sins that you've let creep into your life without considering the dire ramifications. Instead, you rationalize their presence and claim your weakness as a valid excuse. We've gotten so used to having these sins in our lives that we don't even consider them sin any longer—we consider it "just me being me." But it doesn't take long to discover that those behaviors are in fact sin when we take a look at God's Word. Michael has a quote that goes like this: "Nothing personal, but I need less of you/me and more of Jesus. *Let's not replace dying to self with 'being the best me I can be.'*"

In order to Unstuff our minds we've got to be willing to take a look at the sins we've accepted as just a part of life and then **determine to walk away from them and walk toward the Cross**. There is help for this great task, so don't get overwhelmed by the impossibility of it all; God will help you. "By his divine power, God has given us everything we need for living a godly life. We have received all of this by coming to know him, the one who called us to himself by means of his marvelous glory and excellence. And because of his glory and excellence, he has given us great and precious promises. These are the promises that enable you to share his divine nature and escape the world's corruption caused by human desires" (2 Peter 1:3-4).

Life on the Road, Day 49

Hayley: Envy has reared its ugly head. At each campground I continue to see bigger and better motor homes than ours. And today we got to go into one. A young couple with a three-year-old boy invited Addy and me over to play. *Wow* is all I can say. Such luxury. Their "bus," as they called it, has three slides—those parts of the coach that slide out, expanding the width of the rooms. It was like a real home compared to ours with no slides. And I have to confess I coveted the space. So we went across the freeway to the motor coach factory to look at something bigger. After oohing and aahing over the magnificent vehicles, we drove home, saying, "Look how easy it is to think you need more. We've only lived in our motor home for forty-nine days, and now we want to 'move up'? Just in case we thought we were holier than we are, here's a wake-up call." Tonight we came home and thanked God for revealing to us our need for only what we have and nothing more.

THERE IS FREEDOM FROM ALL THE STUFF IN YOUR LIFE THAT CORRUPTS YOU. We can—all of us—get out from under our own human desires and be free to live only for God's desires. That is the only way to true peace, hope, and joy.

◆ ◆ ◆

some final stuff

1. Time for the most basic question when it comes to mind stuff: Is God all you need, or is a supplement required? In other words, do you need more than God alone, or can you exist happily with only him as your source of pleasure and gratification?

2. The next time you're tempted to say, "There's not enough," what will you do to embrace an abundant life instead?

3. What is some of the messy stuff that needs to come out of your heart and mind? What's one step you can take toward becoming free from that this week?

Tweet ♪

Nothing personal, but u need less of u and more of Jesus. Let's not replace dying to self with "being the best you u can be." #Unstuff

COMFOR

MONEY

MONDAY NIGHT FOOTB

JUNK MOTOR HO

SATION DER

SUBSCRIPTION

CLOSETS TIME-SHA

EAT PANEL

SAFETY VACATION CA

SLEEPS KIBO

SSONS CREDIT CA

URE

ES FOOD

IBLE STUDY ROMAN

CER PRACTIC

VIDEO GAMES

MILY CAR

EXERCISE IMA

JEWELRY

SHOE

SION

COUPONS TWITTER GOSS

MAGAZI

BODY STUFF

Section Three

unstuff.org

"Each of you will control his own body and live in holiness and honor." 1 THESSALONIANS 4:4

"Many are lured to their doom by their appetites."
—HERBERT SHELTON

Stuff has an impact on more than our wallets and our minds; it can take its toll on our bodies as well. Since the body is the vehicle by which we acquire, ingest, use, and otherwise consume stuff, it is often the victim of our desire for more stuff than we physically need. Before the Fall, in the Garden of Eden, life was lived in balance. Adam and Eve must have enjoyed all the stuff God had given them—animals, plants, water, fruit. They had no need to hoard, no Joneses to keep up with. When they were hungry, they reached up and grabbed a plum or pear. When they were tired, they lay down and slept. They didn't buy stuff, care for stuff, or collect stuff. The stuff in their lives existed for the purpose of meeting their needs. This was life at its purest. But then **that fateful day arrived when the humans realized there was something they couldn't have, something they had never tried but that looked very good to them**. And suddenly they were no longer content with their idyllic life in paradise; they wanted more. They wanted to be like God (Genesis 3:5). So they ate. And from that moment on, their bodies and the bodies of the entire human race after them would make gods out of stuff.

Stuff can be of great benefit to us, but when the stuff becomes essential in our minds, the next step is that it starts corrupting our bodies. The human body is not made for excess. ***There are any number of health conditions that stem from our overindulgence***, either in the area of ingestion or habits. From heart conditions to stomach conditions to nerve conditions, all the systems of our bodies are keenly affected by the role stuff plays in our lives.

God designed our bodies perfectly so we could live life to the full. The digestive system helps us get what we need for life and strength as food is digested, absorbed, and evacuated from our bodies with very little effort on our part. Our nervous system was designed to alert us to need, danger, and pain and to help guide us to safety. Our respiratory system works effortlessly to bring us the oxygen our bodies need for life. But with our fascination with stuff comes body problems—the more stuff, the more problems. Excess food brings digestive problems. Excess activity brings muscular and even endocrine problems. Excess dieting leads to malnutrition. Excess cholesterol leads to heart problems. Excess sunlight leads to burning. **To the human body, excess brings problems.**

> "Don't you realize that your body is the temple of the Holy Spirit, who lives in you and was given to you by God? You do not belong to yourself, for God bought you with a high price. So you must honor God with your body." 1 CORINTHIANS 6:19-20

But there is even more at stake than just the physical here. A person's body is not their own, but the living space of God himself.

Since the body is the temple of God, the value we place on our health speaks to the value we put on the God who inhabits it. *AS BELIEVERS WE CAN NO LONGER CONSIDER OUR BODIES TO BE OUR OWN—THEY BELONG TO CHRIST.* "He died for everyone so that those who receive his new life will no longer live for themselves. Instead, they will live for Christ, who died and was raised for them" (2 Corinthians 5:15). When we no longer live for ourselves, we are released from the desire for excess, since excess has to do with self-gratification. And when we are free from excess, we are free to live for Christ and experience the rich and satisfying life in him that he promises.

> The value we place on our health speaks to the value we put on the God who inhabits it.

***Moderation* is a key word for the believer.** It allows us to enjoy stuff without being destroyed by it. The apostle Paul explained this biblical principle to the Corinthians: "You say, 'I am allowed to do anything'—but not everything is good for you. And even though 'I am allowed to do anything,' I must not become a slave to anything" (1 Corinthians 6:12). And so the key to freedom both spiritually and physically is to release ourselves from the chains of stuff.

Just like wallet stuff and mind stuff, **body stuff can be terribly uncomfortable to confront**. But if we ever want our bodies to be free from the tyranny of stuff, our only option is to face it head-on. If there is something in our lives that is working against the natural health and purity of our bodies, it will never get better if we ignore it, deny it, or claim a complete inability to control it. At the point that we say we are powerless to control ourselves and to act on what we believe to be true, we are giving our self-life more glory and power than the God who lives in us.

But when we refuse ourselves, even at the cost of pleasure and comfort, we give our bodies a fighting chance to be free from the control of stuff and its nasty side effects.

19: Health Conditions

Believe it or not, **many of our health conditions point to a problem with stuff**. Too much stuff can affect the liver, lungs, heart, and kidneys, and it can even play a role in the likes of cancer, hypertension, diabetes, and strokes. That's not to say all illness is due to stuff, but the pursuit of stuff can lead us to emotional stress that over time can lead to illness and even death. We run ourselves ragged, and in the end, what do we have to show for it? An overactive adrenal gland, a worn-out heart, and a failing liver? But as we peel back the layers of stuff, we give ourselves a chance to breathe.

STUFF SICK

Note the relationship between our feelings about stuff and our health:

Physical Symptoms of Too Much	Causes of These Symptoms
Liver problems	Drinking to medicate
Heart issues	Smoking to medicate
Hypertension and stroke	Stressing over stuff
Diabetes, gas, and bloating	Living to eat, not eating to live
Ulcers	Worrying about stuff

TweeT ♪ Exercise and even light activity can help #Unstuff ur mind, spirit, and waistband. Do a little something extra today for your body and soul.

20: Weight Issues

"The simple fact is that more people die in the United States of too much food than of too little."
—DAN GLICKMAN, FORMER U.S. SECRETARY OF AGRICULTURE

What we think about food says a lot about what we think about God. It was food that symbolized the downfall of all humanity in the Garden of Eden. And it is food that has in many ways become the downfall of modern humanity. There are a lot of emotions tied up in the foods we eat. *MOST OF US NO LONGER EAT TO LIVE BUT INSTEAD LIVE TO EAT.* Food is our passion. We eat it with one thing in mind: pleasure. Sure, there are some people who eat with the goal of nourishment, but for the most part, food has moved from a physical requirement to extraneous stuff. It has become our pastime, our addiction, our disorder, and our master. Most of us find it hard to say no to meals we crave, to delicacies that give us the same kind of high that drugs give an addict. We could probably all draw the food pyramid and explain what our bodies need in order to grow healthy and strong, but how many of us live by those guidelines? When we have a hard day, we want to sit down and open a quart of ice cream, eat an entire large pizza, or dig into a dozen chocolate doughnuts. We find it almost impossible to eat three to five servings of vegetables a day. We would rather have something sugary and starchy for dinner than crisp and crunchy (unless it's fried chicken). We love food and all that it does for us. When we are tired, we want comfort food. Had a tough day at work? Comfort food. Watching the game? Comfort food.

But the high doesn't last long. Partaking of the delicacies we desire leads to all kinds of pain—from bloating to gas to intestinal pain to fatigue and uncomfortable weight gain (not to mention spiritual and emotional consequences). Yet despite being intelligent people who understand the cause of the old spare tire and the noxious fumes, we still can't seem to find the strength to turn the boat around and eat a healthier diet.

Food is one of the areas where many of us have allowed sin to creep in as an acceptable part of our daily routines. For most Christians, the thought of a life filled with sexual sin, theft, hatred, or dishonesty disgusts us. But for some reason—maybe it's the tremendous physical gratification or the lack of stigma associated with it—we have settled in comfortably with the sin of a lack of self-control. Just look around the pews at your local church and see how many people there are carrying around unhealthy weight. If we looked around the church and saw that exact number of people smoking cigarettes, would we be as calm? Or what if the same number of people were groping their partners or wearing tube tops, short shorts, and fishnet stockings? Would we be outraged?

When it comes to food addiction, it isn't the food or the pleasure of it that is the sin but the lack of self-control. ***Self-control is a requirement in the life of the believer*** (1 Thessalonians 4:4; 2 Peter 1:5-7). If we are being driven by our physical and emotional desires for food, then we are no longer truly in control. As Paul puts it, we are being controlled by the sin living in us (Romans 7:17). In that case our god is our appetite, and that leads to destruction (Philippians 3:19). This brings us to a biblical term that isn't very popular in the modern church. It is a word that has gone out of fashion, which is ironic since its practice is very popular these days. What we're talking about here is gluttony—the common condition of going to excess in the area of eating or drinking. When we consume more than is required—more food, more calories, more sugar, more saturated fat—we are by very definition gluttons. And if anything can come between God and us, it is the sin of gluttony.

Most of us can't list all three sins of Sodom, that infamous city that was destroyed because of how it lived. So as a refresher, here they are: *PRIDE, GLUTTONY, AND LAZINESS* (Ezekiel 16:49). If we're honest, how many of us are guilty of at least two of these sins ourselves when it comes to our consumption of food? Or how many of us seriously consider the warning of Proverbs 23:2: "If you are a big eater, put a knife to your throat"?

> "Their god is their appetite, they brag about shameful things, and they think only about this life here on earth." PHILIPPIANS 3:19

Why does God's Word make such a big deal of the sin of over-eating? Maybe it's because food can be a silent killer. While it's a requirement for life, unlike, say, porn or murder, it is something that must be done in moderation. Moderation requires a tricky balance, because we have to do the very thing that can destroy us—but in a way that helps us. And so food stuff walks a fine line between slavery and self-control.

As believers, we need to find the strength to **take back our bodies—the temple of God—allowing them to be used for God's purposes and not for self-gratification** (1 Thessalonians 4:7; Titus 3:3-5). Though food addiction is less blatant, it is just as deadly as the more flagrant and flashy sins we hate. It

WHEN WE KILL OURSELVES WITH FOOD STUFF

More than 85 percent of all diabetics are overweight.

More than 70 percent of all heart-related disease is correlated with being overweight and/or obese.

Almost 45 percent of all breast and colon cancer cases are related to obesity and/or being overweight.

More than 30 percent of all gallbladder problems are caused by obesity and/or being overweight.

may not destroy families or send people to jail, but it does slowly destroy the lives it controls.

TWeeT ♪

Supersize your fruits and veggies today. Try a day with no fast food or processed food and see how your body feels. #Unstuff

Hayley

I have always been a big fan of food. I have always indulged way beyond necessity in order to fully enjoy the taste and the experience to the greatest possible degree. After baking a pie, I can easily eat the entire thing in twenty-four hours. There was a time when buying a quart of ice cream meant I would finish it off in two sittings. If food is good, then more of it is better—that has always been my way of thinking.

I can remember spending my days in my cubicle at work daydreaming about food. I literally made it through the day on the hopes and dreams of dinner. It excited me to think about what my next meal would be. I used food for entertainment and fulfillment. I could never get enough, and I never got too much—at least that's what I told myself. As a kid in high school, I went to a drive-through and got pancakes, sausage, and eggs every morning. I would often eat four or five servings of chocolate mousse a night, along with a box of chocolate-covered cookies. And while I was eating, I was satisfied. I felt like life was worth living, and I was living it well.

But over time this indulgence started to take its toll. Of course, I gained weight, but I also experienced other physical side effects. I started to have intestinal problems, skin problems, digestion problems, and allergy problems. I was tired all the time, listless most of the time, and sick a lot. I didn't want to admit it, but food was the culprit. I discovered that I was no longer eating to live but living to eat, and at that point I realized that my allegiances were wrong. The challenges of life were no longer an opportunity to rely on and trust God but were an opportunity to see if food could cure me a lot quicker than God. Food had become my idol. I worshiped it. I needed it. I couldn't live without it.

At that point I decided that I couldn't be a slave to both food and God, and something had to change. So I took control of my body and my life and decided to eat to live. At first it was hard to shift my focus on food from pleasure to sustenance, but over time the rest of my life got better as the symptoms of my food addiction left me. Like an addict in detox, I had a terrible time at the beginning, but with persistence and a desire to please God over myself, I got through to a new life—a life without addiction and without the pain of that addiction. I started to eat what my body needed, and my body was thankful. Food is still pleasurable to me, but I refuse to let it be my hope, my comfort, or my requirement for happiness.

"I seek out a piece of bread instead of seeking the Bread of Life. I fill my life with food in order to avoid filling it with God." —JOE CARTER

"Do not let sin control the way you live; do not give in to sinful desires. Do not let any part of your body become an instrument of evil to serve sin. Instead, give yourselves completely to God, for you were dead, but now you have new life. So use your whole body as an instrument to do what is right for the glory of God. Sin is no longer your master, for you no longer live under the requirements of the law. Instead, you live under the freedom of God's grace." ROMANS 6:12-14

21: Eating Disorders

"Whether you eat or drink, or whatever you do, do it all for the glory of God." 1 CORINTHIANS 10:31

For some of us, especially those who enjoy nothing more than being skinny and controlling our diets, this discussion so far has been glorious. But it's not just overeating that can control us when it comes to food. If being thin controls us—if all we think about is what we can or can't eat, how many calories it is, or how soon we can throw up—we are just as guilty as the glutton of being controlled by something other than God. ***Obsession is tantamount to worship in that it demands all our heart, soul, mind, and strength, and those are parts of us that God demands only for himself*** (Mark 12:30). This may not be a popular notion, but thinking about nothing other than pant size or body fat is sin. At the point of salvation, the body of the believer is no longer an instrument for evil but a temple for the Holy Spirit (1 Corinthians 6:19-20). Eating disorders in no way serve the Holy Spirit; they serve the flesh.

This isn't a condemnation of the thin but an encouragement to know that we don't have to be controlled by a fear of food or of weight gain because God is on the side of health. **God has made a promise to help us to be obedient, and eating healthy is a form of obedience as we care for the bodies God has given us to serve him** (Ephesians 2:10). It is a lie of the enemy to believe that you cannot control your obsessive thoughts about food and the size of your body. God has made a way out of sin (1 Peter 2:24), including the sin of obsession over food.

Those who struggle with anorexia and bulimia can Unstuff their lives when they take a biblical look at the things that overwhelm them, such as fear, worry, people pleasing, and a desire to control their lives. This can be a difficult process, one that may require professional help from a godly counselor. But when individuals struggling in this area decide to no longer allow anything to come between them and God, they can be free of their food stuff and become healthy and devoted to God more than to self. We Unstuff our lives when we come clean with everything that controls us and determine to hand it over to God.

USDA Daily Requirements for a Healthy Diet

Bread and grains: 6–11 servings a day
Fruit: 2–4 servings a day
Vegetables: 3–5 servings a day
Protein: 2–3 servings a day
Dairy: 2–3 servings a day

Tweet ♪

Someone you know is trying to control their life today thru food. Pray they can see that God has them in his hand. #Unstuff

22: Nervous Breakdowns

Nervous breakdowns can come in varying degrees. And whether we actually have one or feel like we are going to have one, the experience can be incapacitating and sickening. While each situation is different, and some are exacerbated by physiological issues, ***THERE IS A COMMON FACTOR AT THE ROOT OF A NERVOUS BREAKDOWN: OUR ANXIETY OVER STUFF.*** It might be the stuff of money, relationships, lack, or fear, but in some way, stuff no doubt plays a starring role.

While a nervous breakdown may begin as a mental condition, it ends up largely affecting our bodies. With it can come insomnia and other sleep problems, and even emotional consequences like withdrawal, confusion, or feelings of worthlessness. Some people suffer so deeply that they hear voices, feel like they are being pursued or watched, and completely lose control of reality.

In addition to the physiological factors that contribute to a nervous breakdown, there is also most likely a problem of faith. That's because **where faith is lacking, there is the opportunity for much stress and strain**. It might come down to a question of whether we have accepted Christ's gift—his peace of mind and heart. After all, he told us, "I am leaving you with a gift—peace of mind and heart. And the peace I give is a gift the world cannot give. So don't be troubled or afraid" (John 14:27).

Tweet ♪

If u have a bad case of nerves, it's from lack of assurance that God's in control: http://ref.ly/Jn14.27;NLT. #Unstuff

23: Insomnia

At first glance, the connection between stuff and insomnia might seem unclear. But the two are actually closely connected. ***At the times when we should be focusing on rest, our minds are instead swirling with stuff.*** Our thoughts are constantly working, racing to figure out what more we need to do or buy or take care of. Insomnia is often the result of stress, worry, or anxiety that comes when life isn't giving us what we had imagined it would.

Certainly there are instances when insomnia is physical or chemical, but most of the time our sleepless nights result from our obsession over things other than God. In order to reverse this trend, **we have to turn our thoughts over to God and learn to let go of our desire for stuff**. As we stop obsessing over things and start putting our minds under the control of the Holy Spirit during the day, our nights will follow suit. Something to consider is your bedtime ritual. If you pray for God's protection during the day, why not pray for it at night? Pray that he would protect your mind and give you the rest you need. And if insomnia should come, promise to take it as a call to intercession rather than a reason to worry.

Tweet ♪

Can't sleep? Why are u reading this? #Unstuff ur mind by changing up ur routine. Turn off talk radio and 24-hr news and reduce your worry.

24: Fatigue/Low Energy

WHEN STUFF TAKES PRIORITY IN OUR LIVES—WHEN IT IS OUR
DRIVING FORCE—IT REQUIRES A LOT OF ENERGY AND GIVES VERY
LITTLE IN RETURN. Sure, it might be exhilarating to buy something
we've wanted for years, but the exhilaration is only temporary. Soon
we need refueling by new acquisitions.

There are two kinds of weariness: the good kind and the bad
kind. The good kind of tired results from a long day of hard work. As
Christians, we may get tired, but we don't have to spend our days
in mental and spiritual exhaustion because we are able to refuel on
the food of God's Word and his presence. The kind of **weariness**
that results from the pursuit of stuff is another matter. It is the soul-
sucking exhaustion that results from humans working through their
own strength rather than God's.

While *fatigue* isn't a sin, it just **might be a symptom that
you are running yourself ragged in the pursuit of stuff**.
When you stop looking for stuff to fulfill you and instead look to
God to do that, your body can be rejuvenated and energized each
morning. His power animates and strengthens you. When we
Unstuff our lives, we can be rid of unwanted fatigue and gain godly
energy (not false energy gained from more stuff), allowing us to live
more joyful, productive, and restful lives.

TweeT ♪

Looking to #Unstuff your body? Get good
energy instead of fatigue! Read the end of
Prov 30:8: http://ref.ly/Pr30.8;NLT.

some final stuff

1. Think about your eating and sleeping patterns. What habits could benefit from a good Unstuff?

2. What are the biggest physical issues you're currently dealing with? What specific steps can you take to improve those areas of your health?

3. What are some of the spiritual implications of what happens with your body?

> "Give me just enough to satisfy my needs."
> PROVERBS 30:8

COMFOR CLUTHE

MONEY SEX

MONDAY NIGHT FOOTBA

JUNK MOTOR HO

SATION DER

SUBSCRIPTION

CLOSETS TIME-SHA

TION EA PANEL

SAFETY VACATION CA

SLEEPS SKI BO

SSONS CREDIT CAR

URE

ES FOOD

IBLE STUDY ROMAN

CER PRACTI

VIDEO GAMES

MILY AME CAR

UT

EXERCISE IMA

JEWELRY

SHOE

SION

COUPONS TWITTER GOSS

MAGAZIN

LOVE STUFF

Section Four

What's Love Got to Do with Stuff?

Love stuff is the stuff that affects our relationships—the way we give love, the way we receive it, and the way we think about it. Our human attempts to get love can fill up our lives with everything but the very thing we are looking for: more love. *MOST OF THE STUFF IN OUR LIVES MEANT TO BUILD LOVE FROM AN EARTHLY PERSPECTIVE IS REALLY LIKE JUNK FOOD: IT HAS A LOT OF EMPTY CALORIES AND NO NUTRITIONAL VALUE.* But stuff never has the payoff of genuine love. Sure, in the short term it might have a similar sensation to love. It might give us the same kind of warm, fuzzy feeling inside or even send goose bumps across our arms, but stuff doesn't have the same reward as genuine love. Instead, it corrupts love until it's lifeless, empty, and sick.

If we're honest, **we'll admit there are times when we substitute stuff for love and call it a day**. In fact, we even use the same words: "I just love those shoes!" or "I'm in love with the new Camaro." We love everything from Big Macs to houses, and in a lot of instances, that love is so overwhelming, so alluring, that in the end it's all the love we have left. Listen, you can polish your Mercedes all day long with tender loving care, but at the end of the day it's not going to wrap its fenders around you and say, "I love you."

Stuff is wonderful—essential, even—but at some point all of us have let it get in the way of love. We have let it crowd out love, smother it, or destroy it altogether. As with everything, there is a balance to be attained. If the love in your life isn't where you want it to be, then it might be time to Unstuff your love.

Compared to mind stuff and body stuff, love stuff is often less obvious to identify in ourselves. **The symptoms of love stuff can be hard to quantify and difficult to immediately diagnose as a problem.** Love stuff is often stuff we consider to be good—genuinely loving, even. We often make mistakes in love out of a desire to please and serve, but we have to make sure what we're talking about is real love, not an imitation.

RELATIONSHIP STUFF AUDIT

Consider your relationships to see if love stuff is something you struggle with:

1. Which word more accurately reflects your life?
   (a) restful
   (b) busy

2. When it comes to community, how would you describe yourself?
   (a) active and involved
   (b) not really involved

3. Which of the following reflects your view of others?
   (a) I resent others for their lack of effort.
   (b) I think other people need to rest more.

4. What is your perspective on strangers?
   (a) I am open to meeting and welcoming them.
   (b) I'm concerned about acquaintances but not strangers.

5. Is there never enough time in the day or plenty of time to connect with the people in your life?

25: No Time for Relationships

Are there relationships in your life that are suffering because you just don't have enough time? Do you find yourself so busy that you can't go out to lunch with friends, take vacations, play with your kids, or just sit and enjoy the day? The pace of life can sometimes get so out of control that it feels like there's nothing we can do about it. We run from activity to activity just to keep going. We microwave our foods because we don't have time to do anything else. We say things like, "I've been meaning to do that—I've just been too busy." And the things of eternal value suffer. If you feel that way, you're not alone: more than half of Christians around the world feel their busy schedule hinders them from spending more time with God.[4]

BUSYNESS IS A CRUEL TASKMASTER. It never creates good memories, it never develops relationships, and it certainly never expresses love to our loved ones. Instead, it does its best to hijack those meaningful moments in our lives. Nope, busyness doesn't have much of a payoff except to keep our stuff coming in, cleaned up, organized, or protected. Because when you think about it, a large part of our busyness has to do with stuff. We want to keep all our stuff—house, cars, boats, toys, and activities—so we work hard to pay the bills. And we want to buy new stuff, so we work even harder. We want to take care of the stuff we already have, so we spend much of our days cleaning it, straightening it, and organizing it. We fill our schedules with all kinds of activities like sports, hobbies, and church events, and suddenly there's more stuff to do than there is time in the day. Of course, all that stuff isn't inherently bad—some of it is very beneficial and builds lasting relationships. But when there's more stuff than time, something or someone suffers, and most often it isn't just us, but also those we love.

Like it or not, stuff impacts our love lives. And a lot of the time

stuff degrades a relationship until it becomes merely a cheap imitation of love. Some parents buy the lie that their kids need all the stuff they ask for, and for them long hours and hectic schedules mean love. But the kids end up getting what they don't really need instead of what they do need, which is time with their parents. Some people would say it's not quantity that matters but quality. But just ask a ten-year-old if she'd rather have a high-quality square of fine chocolate imported from France or a big bag of Hershey's chocolate kisses. What do you think will win? Or imagine trying to have a romantic relationship with someone who only dropped by a few times a year when it fit into his schedule. Sure, he spent lavishly during those eight weekends a year with you, but no self-respecting woman would settle for an arrangement like that.

Quantity trumps quality every time. Love is built on time spent, not on how good the time is. Time spent sitting on the back porch, watching the birds fly by, cuddling on a hammock, or just walking around the neighborhood builds lasting, loving memories. But how many times does busyness get in the way of those moments?

If life is too busy—if we wish we had more time, more love, more relationships—then *IT MIGHT BE TIME TO CONSIDER THE PULL OF STUFF IN OUR LIVES*. What stuff can be eased up on? What stuff can be let go of altogether?

BUSYNESS INVENTORY

Do you feel too busy to spend time with those you love?

Do you feel too busy to spend time serving someone in need?

Do you feel too busy to spend time praying to the God you worship?

What can you eliminate in order to slow down and have time to love?

Hayley

We decided long ago that family time was more important than cleaning time. So after dinner we don't run into the kitchen and do dishes. We stack them in the sink, and then we all go into the family room to play, talk, or just spend time with each other. When Michael's not traveling, he works most days until 5:00 or 6:00, so we consider those final few hours after he's done working really valuable—even more valuable than taking care of our stuff. Some people might be cringing right now, thinking, *How disgusting*, but as we wrestled with this, we had to decide what's more important: our obsession with cleanliness or our relationship with our family.

There are a lot of activities we unconsciously make more important than those we love. For a lot of women it's cleanliness; for men it might be work or rest from work. It might be a hobby or a sport or a TV show or even a church commitment. But **the two greatest commandments don't have anything to do with the stuff in our lives, but rather with the relationships in our lives**. "Love the LORD your God with all your heart, all your soul, and all your mind. . . . Love your neighbor as yourself" (Matthew 22:37-39).

Tweet

When u r 2 busy 4 relationships, ur saying that loving stuff is more important than loving people. What r u going 2 do about it? #Unstuff

"Search for peace, and work to maintain it." 1 PETER 3:11

26: Isolation

We love our stuff, and we use it to define us, to make our mark, to complete us. ***Stuff gives us the illusion that we can do life on our own***—a false sense of security that comes with the accumulation of more and more. Besides, not having to rely on anyone for anything is the ultimate way to ensure that our stuff remains ours. While individuality and independence have their place, they can also lead to negative consequences when they stand against the belief that we are the "body of Christ" (1 Corinthians 12:12-20).

We are meant to live in fellowship with one another as one body, not separate from each other. When the drive for individuality and independence trumps the goal of unity, the most obvious result is a sense of isolation. And **the more stuff we acquire, the more isolated we become**. The advancement of technology has given us the impression that we don't need each other as much as we used to. Where people once needed the rest of the community for physical survival, now all we need is an Internet connection. Where families used to come together each night around the dinner table after a long day to enjoy a good meal and conversation, now we nuke our food, eat in front of the TV, and afterward run off to do our own thing. We can telecommute and never form work relationships. We can buy everything we need online and never leave the house. We can even have food delivered and be quite content in our isolation.

So why don't we reach out to form lasting bonds with other people? Most of us would say it's because we're too busy, too occupied, or too tired. If we looked below the surface on that issue, we'd recognize that we're running ourselves ragged in the pursuit of stuff. We have bills to pay, appointments to make, and to-do lists to keep up with, and over time this stuff habit results in

THE ANATOMY OF A COMMUNITY

How many people do you communicate with online each day?

How many people do you communicate with over e-mail each day?

How many people do you communicate with by phone or text each day?

How many people do you communicate with in person each day?

an isolation that separates us from the very people we were meant to love and serve.

THE MORE STUFF WE HAVE, THE LESS WE FEEL OUR NEED FOR COMMUNITY AND FELLOWSHIP WITH OTHERS—AND THE MORE WE SUFFER AS A RESULT. When the body of Christ fails to function as a true community, the people of God also suffer. It's high time we Unstuffed.

Life on the Road, Day 57

Hayley: Life in community is amazing. When you live in an RV park, your space is shared closely with many other people. And while as Americans we love our big houses and big lots, there is something right about living close to others. As Addy and I walked through the park today, we saw kids playing on bikes, couples walking around holding hands, and animals resting in the shade. It made my heart happy. Isolation is a natural outcome of bigger and better, but when you downsize, you learn to find contentment and happiness in one another rather than in stuff.

TWeeT ♪

#Unstuff your life of isolation. That includes your 5,000 fb friends. Go talk to strangers today. Have coffee with a possible new friend.

27: Giving Stuff in Place of Love

When we think that stuff is what makes people happy, when we offer stuff as the expression of our love, *we run the risk of letting stuff pollute the love in our lives*. Certainly giving is an essential part of love and faith. We can express love through giving where we see a need, but there is another kind of giving that serves as a substitute for love. We hear this complaint from women who feel like their husbands would rather supply their needs and even their wants than give them their time. We hear the same thing from people who grew up not knowing their fathers because they worked so much. And though to a man, tangible provision might feel like the best way to express love, the truth is that stuff doesn't equal love.

When we use stuff to express our love, we can easily lead those we love to stumble (Habakkuk 2:9; 1 Corinthians 8:9; Ephesians 5:5). In that case, we can do our loved ones a favor by refraining from giving them stuff. **Our goal must be to practice a love like God's, not like the world's**—a love with the goal of holiness, not just happiness. The trouble with the kind of happiness that comes from stuff is that it is fleeting, and it builds our muscle memory so we turn to stuff for what only God can supply: joy, peace, hope, contentment, and comfort.

When we place more value on stuff than it deserves, we slowly erode the genuine love in our lives. Getting stuff can certainly feel like love, but *IN THE BIBLE'S PICTURE OF LOVE, THERE IS NO MENTION OF STUFF* or its value in a relationship. Take a look at these descriptors of love and see where the giving of stuff fits in: "Love is patient and kind. Love is not jealous or boastful or proud or rude. It does not demand its own way. It is not irritable, and it keeps no record of being wronged. It does not rejoice about injustice but rejoices whenever the truth wins out. Love never gives up, never loses faith, is always hopeful, and endures through every circumstance" (1 Corinthians 13:4-7).

Love isn't expressed in the giving of stuff. In fact, even when giving is commanded, it isn't to satisfy indulgence or lust but to meet a need. "They sold their property and possessions and shared the money with those in need" (Acts 2:45). Stuff gets in the way of love when we decide it's the only way to express our love.

The truth is that the people who love you want *you* more than the stuff you give them. So in order to love them more, consider how you can Unstuff your idea of love.

When genuine love becomes more important than the

Michael

This year for Christmas we made an agreement: instead of going out as usual and buying all kinds of gifts to put under the tree, we chose to make coupon books for each other and give those instead. At the end of the day, after the coupon books had been exchanged, we all looked at each other and genuinely said, "This was the best Christmas ever!" The strain of searching for stuff, wrapping stuff, and worrying about getting and giving the right stuff was gone. We enjoyed getting what amounted to time from each other—free back rubs, pizza and a movie, and babysitting time.

simulation of love, we are all set free to enjoy the simple things in life—like time with one another and with God.

TweeT ♪

Kids would rather live in a less expensive house and have more time with their parents. That's because stuff doesn't replace love. #Unstuff

28: Martha Stuff

There is nothing wrong with hard work—it's part of life, and it can have great value. But **when our hard work leads us to the distraction of busyness or to the sin of complaining or becoming bitter, we have a problem**. Most of us are probably familiar with the biblical story of Martha and Mary, but let's recap a bit. Martha and Mary often had guests over to their home, and one of them was a very notable guest, Jesus Christ. They had invited him and all his disciples and some other followers over for dinner, which made for a full house. People were hungry and chores needed to be done, so Martha set out to do them. Mary, on the other hand, sat down to listen and learn from Jesus. She wasn't busy—in fact, she wasn't even moving—and that ticked Martha off. As Martha hustled around the house caring for everyone she saw, she noticed her sister not helping her. And the first thing she thought was, *This is not fair!* She boiled over with resentment, and she said something about it to Jesus. Of course we all know his reply—it's forever engraved in history for all to see. Let's take a look at the scene:

> As Jesus and the disciples continued on their way to
> Jerusalem, they came to a certain village where a woman

named Martha welcomed him into her home. Her sister, Mary, sat at the Lord's feet, listening to what he taught. But Martha was distracted by the big dinner she was preparing. She came to Jesus and said, "Lord, doesn't it seem unfair to you that my sister just sits here while I do all the work? Tell her to come and help me."

But the Lord said to her, "My dear Martha, you are worried and upset over all these details! There is only one thing worth being concerned about. Mary has discovered it, and it will not be taken away from her." (Luke 10:38-42)

MARTHA WAS REBUKED FOR BEING "WORRIED AND UPSET OVER ALL [THE] DETAILS." SOUND FAMILIAR? That's the stuff of life that leads us to distraction—the stuff that gets in the way of love. See, it isn't the stuff we have to do but how we react to it, think about it, and feel about it that counts. If Martha had been serving joyfully, turning an ear to hear what Jesus was saying as she prepared his meal, would she have been rebuked? Or would Jesus have been pleased with her service?

Many times we serve with resentment and bitterness toward those who seem to pull less weight than we do. Things like cooking, cleaning, fixing, and helping are good things, but they can get in the way of love when we start keeping score, when we keep track of how much we work compared to how much others work. We can't kid ourselves—our discontentment is no secret to those around us. And that discontentment taints our love relationships and builds all kinds of opportunities for fighting and disagreement.

> "Don't worry about anything; instead, pray about everything." PHILIPPIANS 4:6

Stuff gets between us and God when we measure what others do on a scale against our own service. When we become bitter, we're sinning, plain and simple. **Serving with resentment is wasted service.** The Bible makes it clear that it's not just our service that matters but our attitude as well (Colossians 3:23-25). But serving with an eye only on the one served—God himself—will take away all the stress and strain of our work.

> "Work with enthusiasm, as though you were working for the Lord rather than for people." EPHESIANS 6:7

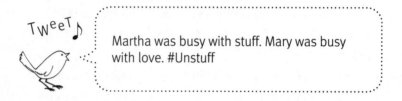

TweeT ♪

Martha was busy with stuff. Mary was busy with love. #Unstuff

29: Sexual Addiction

Sexual addiction, like all other addiction, is a misplaced allegiance to something other than God. It separates us from God by virtue of who or what we're devoting our service to. In Matthew 6:24 we read that we cannot serve two masters, and addiction is no exception. When we are addicted to something, we are no longer slaves to God but to that habit-forming thing. We feel powerless to stop it or to change our ways, so we bow down to our small god and do its bidding. Sexual addiction is particularly heinous because of the importance God gives to the body. Take a look at the following passage:

> You say, "I am allowed to do anything"—but not everything is good for you. And even though "I am allowed to do

anything," I must not become a slave to anything. You say, "Food was made for the stomach, and the stomach for food." (This is true, though someday God will do away with both of them.) But you can't say that our bodies were made for sexual immorality. They were made for the Lord, and the Lord cares about our bodies. And God will raise us from the dead by his power, just as he raised our Lord from the dead.

Don't you realize that your bodies are actually parts of Christ? Should a man take his body, which is part of Christ, and join it to a prostitute? Never! And don't you realize that if a man joins himself to a prostitute, he becomes one body with her? For the Scriptures say, "The two are united into one." But the person who is joined to the Lord is one spirit with him.

Run from sexual sin! *NO OTHER SIN SO CLEARLY AFFECTS THE BODY AS THIS ONE DOES.* For sexual immorality is a sin against your own body. Don't you realize that your body is the temple of the Holy Spirit, who lives in you and was given to you by God? You do not belong to yourself, for God bought you with a high price. So you must honor God with your body." (1 CORINTHIANS 6:12-20, emphasis added)

One way many men and a growing number of women dishonor God with their bodies is through pornography. Porn not only compromises our relationship with God but also the love relationships we are trying to build with people. **If you're married, stuffing yourself with pornography is like eating Spam laced with cyanide and razor blades when you've got steak waiting for you in the next room.** And if you're single, you're just eating that deadly canned meat on the way to the restaurant because of the impatient rumblings of your tummy. Proverbs 5:3-6 says, "The lips of an immoral woman are as sweet as honey, and her mouth is smoother than oil. But in the end she is as bitter as poison, as dangerous as a double-edged sword. Her feet go down to death; her steps lead straight to the grave. For she cares nothing about the path to life. She staggers down a crooked trail and doesn't realize it."

The world would have us believe that our need for stuff is beyond our control, but nothing could be further from the truth. **God gives us everything we need to drive sin out of our lives.** Romans 6:12-14 makes that clear: "Do not let sin control the way you live; do not give in to sinful desires. Do not let any part of your body become an instrument of evil to serve sin. Instead, give yourselves completely to God, for you were dead, but now you have new life. So use your whole body as an instrument to do what is right for the glory of God. Sin is no longer your master, for you no longer live under the requirements of the law. Instead, you live under the freedom of God's grace."

Sin is no longer your master; therefore, there is freedom from addiction.

> "Don't you realize that those who do wrong will not inherit the Kingdom of God? Don't fool yourselves. Those who indulge in sexual sin, or who worship idols, or commit adultery, or are male prostitutes, or practice homosexuality or are thieves, or greedy people, or drunkards, or are abusive, or cheat people—none of these will inherit the Kingdom of God." 1 CORINTHIANS 6:9-10

Tweet ♪

Porn is actually the illusion of stuff. It's stuffing your life with imaginary sin that's still sin. #Unstuff emptiness; grace is waiting.

30: Romance Addiction

There is a lot of stuff that can get in the way of love, but you might never guess that romance could be one of them. Romance, after all, is the fuel of love. It's the result of two hearts exploding in unison and excitement, so how could that get in the way of love? Romance is a great perk of love, especially in the heart of a woman, but romance isn't a requirement for love. And the lack of it doesn't spell the absence or disappearance of love. **A lot of times romance gets in the way of genuine love when it becomes the stuff we concentrate on.**

In general, men and women have different ideas about what constitutes romance. *WOMEN TEND TO EQUATE ROMANCE WITH LOVE, WHILE MEN TEND TO USE ROMANCE TO GET LOVE* (or sex). Then once men have gotten what they want, they find no need for further romance. It's like going hunting, shooting the deer, dropping it in its tracks, and then walking up to it and shooting it over and over again. There's no need, right? You've bagged the deer, and it's yours. So why keep hunting it? Men often think they've done their job once they've snagged the woman, and then they feel no need to keep working to get her. This might bring sadness to the hearts of millions of women, but the truth is that romance isn't a necessity for love or for the man you love. And if you decide it is, you're essentially saying that stuff is more important than love.

Of course we aren't saying that men can get off scot-free and not show love to their wives. When a man loves a woman, he finds out what pleases her, and he attempts to give a portion of it to her. In that case, romance is a great gift from a man to a woman. But it becomes a stumbling block to a relationship—and to faith—when it is demanded. **Remember 1 Corinthians 13:5: love doesn't demand its own way.** And so when romance is a demand, it destroys love.

We would be remiss at this point if we didn't address the occasional case of a relationship where the man wants more romance than the woman. When this happens, especially with the "nice guy," the same thing is true. No one—men or women—should demand stuff from a loved one in order to claim love. If your relationship lacks romance and you are trying hard to generate it, then it's time to back off and understand the true meaning of love. ***When the stuff of romance is overly important to us, it puts a stranglehold on genuine, unconditional love.***

Tweet ♪

> True romance is a God who dies on a cross for ppl who will never deserve it. #Unstuff your life of being the deserving princess (or prince).

31: Selfishness

When we focus too much on our stuff, we leave the door wide open for the habit of selfishness to creep in. **The more we focus on our own stuff, the less room we have to focus on other people and their suffering.** There might be a family down the

---

HOW TO TELL IF ROMANCE IS AN IDOL

Do you frequently find yourself wishing your significant other acted more like chick-flick material?

Do you hold people in your life to impossible ideals when it comes to relationships?

Do you find yourself disappointed when holidays roll around and that special person in your life didn't deliver the way you'd hoped?

street who can't afford to pay their mortgage, but we miss out on the opportunity to help them because our eyes are fixed on our need for new carpet or a bigger bedroom suite. When we concentrate on our desire for more stuff, we lie to ourselves about what we really need and about our responsibility to help others.

Our selfishness affects not only our neighbors but also our relationship with God. ***THE MORE MYOPIC WE BECOME, THINKING ONLY ABOUT OUR OWN STUFF, THE LESS USEFUL WE ARE TO GOD,*** who wants to use us as his hands and feet to the world. This disconnect from the true purpose of life separates us from God, putting something between us that wasn't meant to be there (Luke 9:23).

When we occupy ourselves with seeking our own pleasure, it becomes almost a full-time job. From what we wear to what we drive to what we eat and where we live, it's all about making decisions based on pleasing ourselves. But pleasing ourselves never works out as planned. When our main goal is our own happiness, we end up failing at the very thing we're trying to accomplish.

Tweet ♪

The main goal of selfishness is our happiness above all others'. #Unstuff selfishness today by saying, "You pick; you decide."

32: Irritability with Interruption

When we feel like pulling someone's hair out because we got interrupted from what we were doing, we are reacting based on stuff rather than love. Love isn't irritable; it is patient and kind (1 Corinthians 13:4-5). When real love has been sacrificed at the altar of your belongings, the result is almost always sin. In these situations, **our obsession with the stuff at hand paralyzes our ability to love**

the one who interrupts. When irritability strikes, it is impossible not only to love but to complete the task that was interrupted. So our irritability does no good either to ourselves or to the interrupter.

Life isn't really about the stuff at hand but about the way we love God and serve others. C. S. Lewis puts it this way: "The great thing, if one can, is to stop regarding all the unpleasant things as interruptions of one's 'own,' or 'real' life. *The truth is of course that what one calls the interruptions are precisely one's real life—the life God is sending one day by day*; what one calls one's 'real life' is a phantom of one's own imagination."

When stuff becomes more important to us than it was meant to be, we miss out on real life, on the purpose God had in mind for that moment.

Tweet ♪

> An obsession with the stuff at hand can turn interruptions into irritability. #Unstuff your life by loving the interrupter.

Life on the Road, Day 69

Hayley: Today at the campground we had four little kids from across the campground sitting around our table doing crafts. Addy loved having little friends to play with, and we loved being able to share our day and our art supplies with the "neighbor" kids. This would never happen at our house because we live in such a secluded area. There is a great deal to be said about living close to others, even if they are strangers. They don't stay that way for long.

some final stuff

1. What three relationships are causing you the most sleepless nights right now? What love stuff do you need to Unstuff?

2. Carve out a solid chunk of time this week to spend with someone you love—possibly someone you haven't been giving due time to lately.

3. What's one thing you need to get rid of or cut back on so you can work on a friendship or a relationship with a family member?

COMFORT

MONEY

MONDAY NIGHT FOOTB

JUNK MOTOR HO

CATION DER

SUBSCRIPTION

CLOSETS TIME-SHA

PANEL

SAFETY VACATION CA

SLEEP SKI BO

SSONS CREDIT CAR

TURE

FOOD

BIBLE STUDY ROMAN

CER PRACTIC

VIDEO GAMES

MILY FAME CA

EXERCISE IMA

JEWELRY SHOE

TWITTER GOSS

COUPONS MAGAZI

WORSHIP STUFF

STUFF

Section Five

unstuff.org

As followers of Christ, our worship is what defines us. We worship the one true God, the God of Abraham, Isaac, and Jacob. We believe that Jesus is the Son of God and that he died on a cross and rose again and that because of his sacrifice, we are saved. We believe that the Bible is the inspired Word of God and that it teaches us how to live godly lives by **revealing who God is and what the Cross was for**. We believe that prayer is an essential part of life and that giving to and serving those in need is how we love God and people. We worship God in action and in song. We think about him as we drive to and from work. We talk about him with our friends, and we rely on him for our eternal hope. We are believers, Christ-followers, Christians. And, supposedly, some 82 percent of the population of the United States identifies with us.[5]

Those of us who call ourselves Christians go to church—if not consistently, then at least on major holidays. We define ourselves by our faith, and for the most part, it affects all aspects of our lives. Truth be told, though, there are times we slip up, times we aren't as faithful as we want to be, times we doubt that God will help us. We want more of him in our lives, but sometimes the Bible overwhelms us and we don't know where to start or what to do. *WE BELIEVE IN PRAYER, BUT WE ARE MOSTLY PRAYERLESS, UNINSPIRED, AND TIRED.* We want to make a difference in the world, but there just isn't enough time, enough money, or enough energy to go around.

We have mountaintop moments—spiritual successes and times of great progress in our faith—but that's the exception, not the rule.

There are significant seasons when we are tired, thirsty, and empty, and we find ourselves wishing we had more of him. We want more peace, more hope, more rest, more joy, but we can't seem to muster the strength to find it. We watch our friends and hear about their "testimonies" and "praises," and we wonder why our lives aren't as blessed as theirs. We are tempted, we sin, we mess up, and we get distracted, but we come back to him—eventually. And we thank God for his grace and his never-ending pursuit of us. **We wish we were more like him—more consistent, more faithful, more passionate about our love for him.**

Worship is a barometer of our faith. The way we worship tells us how things are going in our relationship with God. ***We tend to decide how we are doing spiritually based on how well we worship.*** We may get frustrated with ourselves because we try to pray but just don't know what to pray about, or because we want to get up early to study God's Word but we just can't seem to get out of bed. We say, "I wish I were closer to God. I wish I could hear him more." If that's you, you're not alone. We are all human and weak, and we all need more of him.

What if you could have more—more of him, more faith, more prayer, more energy to study? Would you take it? Would you be the first to say, **"I'm so in"?**

What's Worship Stuff?

WORSHIP STUFF IS EVERYTHING THAT GETS IN THE WAY OF OUR WORSHIP. It's the stuff that comes between us and God and obstructs our view of and even our access to the Father. When we have worship stuff in our lives, we find ourselves too uninspired, too tired, too bored, too unsure to experience genuine worship. We aren't where we want to be, and that bothers us, but we don't have any idea how to get our faith out of the rut it's stuck in.

Not only can worship stuff get in the way between us and God, but it can even become a little god in itself. Right now you might be thinking, *What? I don't worship anything other than God—that's idolatry!* But just humor us for a minute. Is there anything in your life that controls you more than God? Are there things that keep you from true worship? Things that interrupt your prayer time, study time, church time, serving time? Are there things in your life you know you should say no to, but you just don't have the power to do so? If so, it may be time to Unstuff your worship.

33: Obsession

The idolatry of obsession happens when anything other than God persistently occupies our thoughts. ***When we obsess, the object of our obsession becomes the very definition of an idol.*** And it goes without saying that an idol gets in the way of our worship of God.

> Idolatry: any immoderate attachment or devotion
> to anything other than God

One of the ways stuff becomes an idol is when we give it credit for doing things that only God should get credit for. The first love in our life is meant to be God (Deuteronomy 6:4-5), but a lot of times stuff creeps into that position and dethrones God in our hearts. God often gives us his comfort, hope, provision, peace, and joy in the form of stuff, but so often we give the thanks or credit to the stuff itself rather than to God. This stuff then becomes our idol—something that receives our devotion. It goes something like this: "Yesterday was awful—I had the worst day at work and I got into a fight with my best friend. But when I got home, I had a pint of rocky road, and all my troubles faded away. It was like a wave of calm came over me. And all was right with the world again." In this scenario, the ice cream fills in the place of God; it comforts, takes away the burden, and gives peace. These things should be gifts from God's hand, not a dairy product. In the book of Exodus, God tells us something important about his character: he is jealous. He doesn't like competition or having other gods vie for his place. Of these little gods, he says, "You must not bow down to them or worship them, for I, the Lord your God, am a jealous God who will not tolerate your affection for any other gods" (Exodus 20:5). God doesn't like rivals. Lesser gods out there are trying to compete for the affection of his people, offering them the very things God promises and enticing them to be content with less than God himself. When we have these idols in our lives, our worship suffers. Even if we desire all our worship to be on the big-G God, the little-g gods pull us in another direction.

A SURE SIGN OF IDOLATRY

If you're struggling with greed, chances are good you have a problem with idolatry. When we can't get enough stuff, we make stuff the object of our worship. And greed isn't just about money. We can be greedy for someone else's life, greedy for the entire box of doughnuts, greedy for all the attention of a friend or coworker. And that greed has severe consequences for our lives and worship: "A greedy person is an idolater, worshiping the things of this world" (Ephesians 5:5). Greed impacts not only our faith but also our eternity: "You can be sure that no immoral, impure, or greedy person will inherit the Kingdom of Christ and of God" (Ephesians 5:5).

When stuff becomes our obsession or idol, it makes its way to the driver's seat and ends up controlling us. When we do something we don't want to do and then say something like, "I just can't control myself," or, "I can't help it," or, "I'm totally addicted to _____," we voice the control that stuff has over us. It might feel irresistible. We want to do what is right, but we can't. We don't want to do what is wrong, but we do it anyway (Romans 7:18-19). Sound familiar? We all have worship stuff that gets in the way from time to time. We have trouble praying and studying, and we get bogged down with fear, worry, and stress. We start believing God is distant and can't hear us. But when this becomes a persistent pattern, when we feel like we can no longer control our behavior, we start moving into the realm of addiction.

> "Those who are dominated by the sinful nature think about sinful things, but those who are controlled by the Holy Spirit think about things that please the Spirit. So letting your sinful nature control your mind leads to death. But letting the Spirit control your mind leads to life and peace. For the sinful nature is always hostile to God. It never did obey God's laws, and it never will. That's why those who are still under the control of their sinful nature can never please God." ROMANS 8:5-8

What controls you? If it isn't God, then it is your idol.

Not sure if you have an obsession? Then check out the list of idols on page 131 and see if any of them have mastered you. We have divided them into what we call light idols and dark idols. The light idols are those *THINGS THAT ARE USUALLY GOOD, BUT WHEN THEY LEAD US TO OBSESSION, THEY QUICKLY BECOME IDOLATRY.* The dark idols are things that are sin in and of themselves—the things we typically think of when we talk about idols or addictions. The dark idols may seem more obvious, but we have to remember that both types of idols are capable of being our little gods. Giving anything control of our thoughts and actions is sin, whether the thing is intrinsically good or bad.

Are you willing to give control of your life to God, doing whatever he commands, even at the expense of your little gods that demand so much of your time and mind?

Hayley

My name is Hayley, and my idol is beauty. I love looking at beautiful things. I want fine furniture, nice drapes, good bedding. I want a room with a view, a booth with a view, and an office with a view. For a long time I believed that I couldn't do my job without beauty around me. I write books that teach people about God and his role in their lives, and for years I told myself that I couldn't do that unless everything was just right. I needed inspiration. I needed a pasture to gaze on or a lake to stare at to get the creative juices flowing. I was so convinced of this that I wouldn't work unless all the conditions around me were just right. It became my obsession—and my prison. I was controlled by my environment. But after having our daughter, I realized that I could do a lot of things without the beauty I'd thought I needed. Soon I was working wherever I could find a semi-quiet spot to work. Whether I was staring at a sunrise or a blank wall, I wrote. I wrote about God, his truth, and his Word, and my work didn't suffer without the beauty I used to require. There is nothing wrong with a beautiful environment, of course, but when it becomes a requirement or an obsession, as it did in my life, it becomes an idol.

Light Idols

Family
Friends
Marriage
Love
Romance
Ministry
Happiness
Comfort
Food
Eating healthy
Losing weight
Staying fit
Shopping
Talking
Sleeping
Being perfect
Being responsible
Being successful
Being in control
Being well-liked
Looking good
Sports
Music
Hobbies
Patriotism
Morality
Cleanliness
Safety
Busyness

Dark Idols

Fear
Worry
Self-condemnation
Sexual immorality
Superstition
Cutting
Purging
Starving
Habitual indecision
Complaining
Astrology
Gossip
Revenge
Drugs
Unforgiveness
Guilt
Alcoholism
Gambling
Porn
Laziness
Hatred
Materialism

Each us has a favorite idol—something that gets in the way of worshiping the one true God. It isn't as though we go out to an idol shop, scour the shelves for our favorite idol, pay for it, and then take it home to sit on the little altar set up in the living room. If only they were that easy to spot. No, **our idols sneak up on us**. They grow out of our affection for stuff and become an obsession. Personally speaking, we consider ourselves recovering idolaters. Like alcoholics or drug addicts, we know we still have the tendency to bow down to our idols, so we are never completely free from the need to guard ourselves against them.

Michael

My name is Michael, and my idol is solitude. I love being alone or being left alone. Come Super Bowl Sunday, I would rather create a huge gastronomical spread for myself and watch the game in peace than invite a bunch of people over—or worse, go to someone else's house and watch the game. I married a woman who wants to spend every waking moment with me if possible. That was God's first act of breaking me. Then came my daughter, who is like my wife times ten. It's not surprising, then, that my idol is based on one of God's first observations about the creation he called man: "It is not good for the man to be alone" (Genesis 2:18). And I know that's right, because by myself, without my wife and daughter, I won't learn patience or compassion. Without my friends, I won't learn hospitality or friendship that extends beyond politics and NFL affiliations. Solitude has its time and place; even Jesus was known to seek it out. But I can't let it become my comfort or an escape from the lessons of life and holiness that God wants me to learn through others.

T͟w͟e͟e͟T ♪

> #Unstuff persistent thoughts that aren't of the mind of God. Don't analyze them; throw them out. God hates idols, and u should too.

34: Wanting to Be Comfortable

If we could survey the population of all believers living in the Western world, we are confident we would find that for 95 percent of them, comfort would be one of their top goals. Whether we realize it or not, most of us make our decisions based on the degree of comfort we can or can't expect. From where we sit in a restaurant to what we eat and how we eat it to where we live and work and spend our free time, we focus on our own comfort. When we decide where to go to church, we often base it on what is comfortable to us. We determine who to talk to based on how comfortable we feel around them. Now being comfortable isn't a sin—it's actually a neutral

---

DO YOU WORSHIP AT THE ALTAR OF COMFORT?

How did you decide what city to live in?
How did you decide what home to live in?
How did you decide what clothes to wear today?
How did you decide what you'd eat today?
How did you decide what people you'd talk to today?
How did you decide what temperature to set the thermostat at?
How did you decide what you'd spend your free time doing today?
How much does your comfort influence your decisions?

thing. But **comfort becomes a problem when it keeps us from obeying God's Word**. Most often the worship stuff that gets between us and God has to do with choosing comfort or choosing to avoid its opposite: discomfort. Addicts keep using because it's too uncomfortable to stop. Gossips keep gossiping because it feels comfortable.

Tweet ♪

Our culture is one of comfort and envy. Next time ur at a restaurant, ask for the worst table and watch the server's head explode. #Unstuff

Life on the Road, Day 75

Michael: Life together is significantly better than life on my own. I'm starting to think that finding a way to continue to work in close proximity to my family is the way to go. While other men may enjoy going away from home to work, I'm finding the opportunities for interaction, communication, and play are a wonderful addition to my life. It has been an adjustment, but it is teaching me that the important should never be sacrificed on the altar of the urgent. If our heavenly Father is never too busy to be interrupted, why should my daughter have less access to me?

35: Not Knowing Enough about God's Word

As believers, most of us know it's essential to know God through knowing his Word. But how many of us feel like we just don't know enough about what it says? Maybe we know the basics, enough to get us saved, but don't ask us about the tricky stuff. We don't have a clue. Sure, we'd love to know more—to be wiser and quicker and able to cite a verse to a friend in need—but *WE JUST DON'T KNOW THE BIBLE WELL ENOUGH*. There's so much to it and so little time—where would we start?

For a lot of us, the Bible feels too big and overwhelming, so we skim over it. We flip around, reading a bit here and there but never really studying it. We know there should be more time devoted to it, more study given to it, but how? Where do we start? Unfortunately, what often holds us back is our desire to be comfortable. We don't control ourselves because it's more comfortable to just let ourselves go. We take the path of least resistance so our comfort stays intact. It's a little like raising kids: it might be easier to just give them the candy they want than to listen to them screaming. But does that ultimately produce the results we're hoping for? Change is within our reach. As daunting as it might seem, **we can know the Bible more than we know it now**. We can get to know God more through it, teach it to others, and offer people its words of encouragement and wisdom. But the first thing we have to do is admit that we are the ones keeping ourselves from knowing what we need to know about Scripture.

In the life of the believer there should be nothing that comes between us and the study of God's Word (Deuteronomy 11:18-21). If you find that you don't know God's Word enough for your liking, then take a look at what keeps you from finding a way to change that. It may be time or it may be fear or it may be your stuff. Whatever it is and however uncomfortable it may

Hayley

When I started to realize there wasn't enough time in the day to devote as much time as I wanted to the study of God's Word, I discovered that my idol of comfort was the problem. It's true—my day was filled with raising a young daughter, and that didn't leave much room for quiet time. The only quiet time was between the hours of 9:00 p.m. and 6:00 a.m. Also known as bedtime. And so up to that point, comfort was winning out, along with that warm bed, especially on those cold mornings. But I decided I didn't want an idol to dictate my obedience in studying God's Word. So I decided to slay the idol by getting up at 4:30 each morning. This was one of the hardest things a sleep addict could do, but it had to be done, or comfort would continue to be the idol that came between God and me.

be to change, it is worth the sacrifice. In doing so, you destroy an idol—an idol that has set itself up as a rival to God.

There is nothing that can keep a person more devoted to God than the study of his Word. **Know that to whatever degree you want more of him, you can have more.** It just requires a dogged devotion to the pursuit of God—and death to the need to be comfortable.

Tweet ♪

I know all 464 words to a Spice Girls song u prob know. There are 111 words in Psalm 1. #Unstuff

36: Prayerlessness

PRAYERLESSNESS IS A SIN MOST OF US ARE GUILTY OF. We pray, but not often enough. We pray, but not boldly enough. We go through most of life on our own strength, apart from God, disconnected and aloof. Then we wonder why our worship suffers and why our souls are so weak. As with reading Scripture, it is usually comfort that is the biggest obstacle between us and a life of vibrant prayer.

We don't get to know God and the power of his Spirit by popping in to say hi occasionally. He doesn't shower his gifts on the casual guest or the once-a-week visitor. But he does give himself to those who relentlessly pursue him (Matthew 7:7-8; Luke 11:5-8). God wants us to know the power of persistence. He wants us to believe he can change things—and pray like we believe it (Matthew 21:22).

> "Keep on asking, and you will receive what you ask for. Keep on seeking, and you will find. Keep on knocking, and the door will be opened to you. For everyone who asks, receives. Everyone who seeks, finds. And to everyone who knocks, the door will be opened." MATTHEW 7:7-8

When stuff becomes more important than praying, we suffer from the sin of prayerlessness. In 1 Thessalonians 5:17, Paul writes that we are to pray at all times—without stopping. How many of us can honestly say that's the case for us? Most of us check in occasionally—maybe as we shower or drive to work. We ask him for help when trouble strikes and to bless our food when company comes over. But we never fully experience the full, amazing power accessible to us through prayer.

Tweet ♪

If you poured several cups of syrup inside your cell phone, would you expect a good connection? #Unstuff your life for better reception.

Prayerlessness is one of the biggest symptoms that worship stuff is getting in the way. Not sure if that's a problem for you? Then think about it this way: **does God get even 10 percent of your time?** Granted, there's no biblical formula for how many hours you should pray each day. But go along with us for a minute and follow this line of thought, just for the sake of perspective. If God did receive 10 percent of your time, he would get more than two hours of your day. Now if you didn't want to consider sleep time as part of your day, then you would give God 10 percent of your 16 hours of awake time, or 1.6 hours of your day. Either way you slice it, giving God and prayer the firstfruits of your day requires a significant commitment.

To be sure, it gets uncomfortable to make time to pray. It's uncomfortable to believe that God wants more of our devotion. But *WHEN COMFORT IS NO LONGER OUR IDOL, WE DON'T CARE IF DEVOTION BRINGS DISCOMFORT ANY MORE THAN THE ATHLETE CARES IF TRAINING BRINGS SORE MUSCLES AND FATIGUE.* In order to grow, we are willing to suffer the growing pains.

> "A desire for God which cannot break the chains of sleep is a weak thing and will do but little good for God after it has indulged itself fully. The desire for God that keeps so far behind the devil and the world at the beginning of the day will never catch up." —E. M. BOUNDS

So how much time is sufficient for prayer? That's a question only you can answer. **How much of God is enough for you? How**

much of your devotion is enough for him? For each of us the answer will be different, but the answer will determine the degree of worship we are willing to allow into our lives.

"As a man prays, so is he." —A. W. TOZER

37: Being Disconnected

At the core of every soul is a drive to know and be known. As human beings in general, and especially as believers, we were made for relationship—both with God and with other people. But many times those relationships are few and far between—or remain at just a surface level. *When we choose a life of disconnection, we allow our focus to be on our fears, our failures, our doubts, and our image instead of on the transforming power of God.*

Some of us are socially unskilled, whether from upbringing, natural inclination, or experience. We fear connecting with people, being uncovered as a fraud, or putting up with people who make us uncomfortable. We accept the lie that we have no control over shyness, that it is just part of our personality. But even if it is a part of our DNA, it doesn't have to remain a part of our lives. Shyness can become an idol when we listen to its murmurings instead of obeying God. **God's command to make disciples (Matthew 28:19) doesn't come with an escape clause, such as "Go and make disciples . . . unless you are too shy."** And his command to love others doesn't allow for a written excuse from our moms claiming shyness as an out from obedience.

One of the dangers of shyness is that it can rob us of feeling accepted and a part of something and can instead make us feel isolated and alone. Studies show that people who lack relationships are more likely to be sick, stressed, and depressed.[6]

Beyond that, there are spiritual consequences to isolation: it makes us less likely to impact the world for God. After all, the world is made up of people, and if people are not our thing, then how will we share God with them?

> According to one survey, shyness affects 48 percent of the population.[7]

FELLOWSHIP IS A REQUIREMENT FOR BELIEVERS. As the writer of Hebrews puts it, "Let us think of ways to motivate one another to acts of love and good works. And let us not neglect our meeting

Hayley

You might not guess this about me when you first meet me, but I am incredibly uncomfortable in crowds. I am shy by nature and would prefer a life of ease, only spending time with good friends and family. But knowing that God's Word is more important than my likes and dislikes, I have made the decision to say no to the comfort I could get from using shyness as an excuse and yes to the challenge of kindness, love, and hospitality. There are times in the middle of a group of people when my shyness threatens to make me sick. I imagine the worst in people, remembering the mean girls of my past, but I make a conscious choice not to let the sins of others control me. So I press on in the face of fear and insecurity, believing that God is more powerful than all the fear and failure in the world. This way of thinking has brought me from debilitating shyness to the freedom of not only loving others but reaching out to them as a person who has something life-changing to offer them.

together, as some people do, but encourage one another, especially now that the day of his return is drawing near" (Hebrews 10:24-25). Don't stop meeting with others, even if that means you have to sacrifice your comfort.

When we put the goals God has for us above our own limiting feelings of self-protection and fear, the worship stuff gets out of the way and true worship begins. If you are shy, consider a life of freedom—and know that others have gone before who have denied themselves and picked up their cross to follow Jesus.

Don't let shyness rob you of God's promises. #Unstuff your life of self-protection and fear, and be bait for Jesus.

38: Laziness

The world we live in has practically made an art form of relaxing, not to mention an entire industry. Laziness is almost seen as a right, not a vice. But there are serious consequences to laziness, not the least of which is spiritual weakness. *In its most basic form, laziness is the pursuit of that which is most comfortable.* For those who are lazy, work is uncomfortable, so they seek the comfort of rest. When it comes to the spiritual realm, laziness gets in the way of worship because we use it as an excuse for not pursuing more of God. It comes from a mind set on pleasing self, and its goal is always ease.

But ease isn't all it's cracked up to be. Ease becomes our idol when we tell ourselves, *I'm too tired; I just need to rest,* when there is something God is calling us to step out and do in faith. **Laziness**

controls us when it is the compelling voice in our lives, drowning out the commands of God. When we hear the words, "Go and make disciples," do we find ourselves responding, "Who, me? Too much work!" When we hear the call to serve others, do we say, "What, now? I've got too much to do." And so laziness can get in the way of our obedience to God.

But laziness is rarely called out as a sin anymore. It's not something we confess publicly or even to ourselves. It is most often a hidden idol that pretends to protect us from too much effort but really ends up killing us through inaction. It is on the opposite end of the spectrum from busyness and tries to make itself look better by fighting off its nemesis. *BUT BOTH BUSYNESS AND LAZINESS TAKE OUR FOCUS OFF SERVING GOD AND PUT IT ON SERVING SELF.* If we want our worship to be effective, we need to be able to strike a godly balance between the two.

The book of Proverbs has a lot to say about laziness, for example, "A lazy person is as bad as someone who destroys things" (Proverbs 18:9). Laziness promises rest and recuperation, but what it really does is destroy us. Laziness is the voice in our heads telling us not to go to church today. **It's what keeps us from fellowship, Bible study, prayer, and all kinds of worship opportunities.** If you wish your worship could be more than it is, it might be time to take a look at how laziness is affecting your faith.

TWeeT ♪

Laziness comforts me with the promise of a warm bed and plenty of "me" time. But laziness teaches me nothing about the Cross. #Unstuff

39: Busyness instead of Worship

According to a recent survey, Christian women in the United
States said (1) that they were almost always busy and
(2) that busyness impacted their spiritual walk.[8]

Busyness is one of the more subtle forms of worship stuff, because
it often comes disguised as something good. ***Its strategy is
sneaky but effective: to keep us from the things of
faith by distraction.*** When your life gets too busy, it's your
stuff, not your God, that is occupying your mind. To be busy is to
be unable to respond to the voice of God. It is having a checklist
that has to be followed and allowing nothing to get in the way of its
completion. Jesus did a lot while he walked this earth, but he was
never busy.

If we were to spend the whole day talking with those we love,
serving those in need, or praying to the God we worship, would we
say that we were too busy? Or would we say that we were living a
rich and satisfying life? Of course we can't always spend entire days
in these loving pursuits, but **we need to constantly take stock
of our hearts and our time to determine what we're
placing the most value on**. If life is too busy—if we wish we
had more time with God, more love, deeper relationships—then it
might be time to consider the pull of stuff in our lives and to decide
what can be scaled back or let go.

Time—how we use it and how much we have left
of it—influences how we spend our money.

If the hurry of your day is getting to be too much and you wish
you were less busy, stop wishing and take action. Take a look
at your life and see what stuff compels you to busyness. What

activities are at the root of your hurry and the necessity to go, go, go? *THERE WILL NEVER BE ENOUGH TIME TO CONCENTRATE ON GOD WHEN WE ARE CONSUMED WITH BUSYNESS.* And though we might not believe it, our schedules *are* within our control.

The best way to control a busy life is to learn to say no. **No is not a sin.** When we say no to the good stuff in order to have time for the great stuff, we do ourselves—and our faith—a great service. But we've grown up believing otherwise. As students, many of us participated in several sports, got involved in extracurricular activities, and signed up for anything else we could find in order to make our college applications shine. As adults, our lives may not look much different. We work long hours and rush from commitment to commitment in order to fill our lives with the stuff we deem essential to a happy life. And in the process, we choke out all the happiness we thought would come as a result of our busy schedules.

If you have as much trouble telling yourself no as you do saying no when other people ask you to do something, then consider how the pace of your life would change if you decided you need less. *The more stuff you "need," the busier you are.* But when

Life on the Road, Day 76

Hayley: I just cleaned the coach from top to bottom, and it took me fifteen minutes. At home it would take me at least two hours. Or two days. Wow, I love the simple life! It gives me more time to really enjoy life rather than be burdened by cleaning and organizing. Is that bad? I must admit I like the easy life. Less stuff = less work. Wow, what a concept.

you decide to need less, you are forcibly less busy, and a less busy life is energy-giving. We don't have to work those long hours to get ahead or to get more. Maybe for you that would mean cutting back to part-time work, job sharing, or even working from home in an effort to get the unnecessary stuff out of your life and get back to what really counts. Or it might mean selling everything you own and moving to a foreign country to serve a people group in desperate need of something you can help provide. When our lives mean something in the Kingdom of Heaven, they are less busy and more rewarding. If your busy schedule is an excuse for why you can't spend more time with God, then it's time to Unstuff.

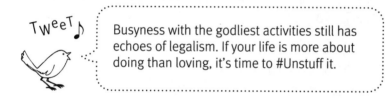

Tweet ♪

Busyness with the godliest activities still has echoes of legalism. If your life is more about doing than loving, it's time to #Unstuff it.

40: Overwhelming Fear

If there is any stuff in your life that you genuinely fear losing—if it keeps you up at night, if you stress over it, if you work to prevent its loss, if you do all you can to protect it—then you may have found your idol. Certainly we are to be careful with the stuff that has been entrusted to us, but when stuff becomes indispensable, sin has crept in.

We know of a woman who had such an overwhelming fear of losing her child that she made herself physically sick. She was certain her daughter would soon die, be kidnapped, or get lost. She was so consumed by the potential loss that she became depressed. Not long after, the child was diagnosed with cancer. This mother's worst fear had come true, and now she was faced with a horrible

Hayley

My fear idol wasn't quite so obvious. For many years I had an unnatural fear of not having enough food. After all, food was my source of comfort and hope. I was addicted to it, but I also had this mixed-up idea that each meal might be my last, so I gorged myself out of the fear of not eating again. At one church retreat, after eating dinner with the group, I sneaked into the kitchen and ate three more servings of food in order to store up just in case that was the last meal of the weekend. Fear of loss overwhelmed me. Fortunately, as I started to identify the idols in my life, I was able to let go of the burden of this little god and begin to trust more in the true God. Believing God over my fear was the best thing I ever did.

prospect: life without her child. As the little girl's condition worsened, the mother's did too. It was like they were both dying. The woman refused to go to church or pray or read the Bible. She said, "If God takes her away from me, I won't trust God anymore."

The tragedy of this story isn't just the loss of a young life but also the way the mother took an amazing gift from God and made it an idol—something that became more important to her than God himself. *SHE WAS SO ATTACHED TO HER IDOL THAT HER FEAR CONSUMED HER AND ULTIMATELY DESTROYED HER FAITH.*

When stuff is our source of comfort, hope, protection, or even salvation, we are likely to be consumed by fear. But fear isn't meant to control the believer. When we renounce our idols and have a healthy fear of the true God alone, we can be set free from all other fear. The fear of God is fear that emboldens; it doesn't paralyze. And while the fear of losing stuff causes weakness, the fear of God is our strength.

"Such love has no fear, because perfect love expels all fear. If we are afraid, it is for fear of punishment, and this shows that we have not fully experienced his perfect love." 1 JOHN 4:18

"You can enter God's Kingdom only through the narrow gate. The highway to hell is broad, and its gate is wide for the many who choose that way. But the gateway to life is very narrow and the road is difficult, and only a few ever find it." MATTHEW 7:13-14

FACE YOUR FEARS

What do you fear most in life?
What things are you terrified to lose?
Confess to God any fear that controls you.

---

some final stuff

1. What in your life is coming between you and genuine worship? What idols have you set up that are more important than God?

2. What in your life is pulling you in a different direction from God?

3. Is your faith stretching you and calling you out of your comfort zone?

TweeT ♪

Fear is the most stupid thing in the world for a believer to hoard. It has no value to us. Do something fear-defying today. #Unstuff

CLOTHE
COMFORT SEX
MONEY'S
MONDAY NIGHT FOOTBALL
JUNK MOTOR HOME
ATION DER
SUBSCRIPTION
CLOSETS TIME-SHAR
TION EAT PANEL
SAFETY VACATION CA
SLEEP SKI BOA
SSONS CREDIT CAR
URE
ES FOOD IA
BLE STUDY ROMAN
CER PRACTIC
VIDEO GAMES
MILY AME CAR
UT EXERCISE IMA
JEWELRY SHOE
SSION
COUPONS TWITTER GOSS
MAGAZIN
OVIE STARS

FUTURE STUFF

STUFF

Section Six

unstuff.org

The Parable of the Three Mansions

Three men each owned a mansion. The first man was aware of all he had been given in life and all others lacked, so he gave away everything he didn't need, keeping only what was essential for life.

The second man was aware of all he had been given and decided it was more than enough for himself and his family, so he sold his mansion and bought a smaller home, giving all the remaining money to people in need. From that day on he wrote a check to charity for the difference between his house payment on his mansion and his payment on his small home.

The third man was aware of all he had been given in life and what others lacked, so he decided to use what he had been given for good. He opened up his house to be used by those in need. His family had room to grow, so they adopted three kids. They turned their basement into an apartment and offered it to families in need who were trying to get back on their feet after losing their housing. And they dedicated their home to the service of those in need, hosting dinner parties and charity events.

Multiplication

> "Those who shut their ears to the cries of the poor will be ignored in their own time of need." PROVERBS 21:13

"Don't forget to do good and to share with those in need. These are the sacrifices that please God." HEBREWS 13:16

When you look at all your stuff, does it give you the sense that your life means something here on earth? Or more significantly, that your life here on earth means something in heaven? *Consumption or stuffing can give the temporary sense that all is well, but it says nothing about life from a heavenly perspective.* When you compare the investment you have in your stuff with the investment you have in heaven, which is greater? The good news is that God can redeem our stuff. We can accept the gifts he gives us but not allow them to stop with us.

Multiplication is the notion that our abundance can be used to supply the needs of many. But in order for this to happen, we have to be strategic about our stuffing and Unstuffing. We can start making a change today to bring relief not only to ourselves but also to others who are less fortunate than we are.

"Beware of harking back to what you were once when God wants you to be something you have never been."
—OSWALD CHAMBERS

Your Stuff List

Remember the list you made in the beginning of this book, "Your Stuff List"? Turn back to page 21 and take a fresh look at your list. Is there anything you'd like to cross out? Anything you used to want more of but don't need anymore? And is there anything you had in your abundance column that you're starting to thin out? If so, cross those out too. *THE GOAL WITH UNSTUFFING ISN'T TO GET RID OF*

*ALL YOUR STUFF—JUST THE STUFF THAT GETS IN THE WAY BETWEEN
YOU AND GOD AND KEEPS YOU FROM LIVING A RICH AND SATISFY-
ING LIFE IN HIM.*

So, looking ahead to the future, what can you do to overcome
your issues with stuff?

1. Admit You Have a Problem

**The first step in overcoming sin is admitting you have
a problem, and it's no different when it comes to stuff.**
Confession is just agreeing with God about our sin and aligning
ourselves with him. When we confess, we say things like, "I'm a
shopaholic, and I don't want to do that anymore," or, "I have a
problem sharing, and I want to change." When we confess, God
gets in the mix with us and forgives us for the errors of our ways,
and then he gets behind us as a much-needed partner in bringing that work to completion (Philippians 1:6). If there is some stuff
between you and God, right now is the time to come clean with it.
After all, it's not like it's going to be a surprise to him. It's just an
act of the will for you.

2. Turn Around

*After you confess your problem, your next step is
to move in the opposite direction. This is called
repentance*, and it's where the change really starts to be notice-
able to the rest of the world (Luke 3:8). Now is the time, in the
words of Thomas à Kempis, to "choose rather to want less, than
to have more." This choice is ours, and it will result in an amazing
return to our first love: God.

3. Give Up Your Self-Life

God isn't selfish; he doesn't keep anything for himself. He lavishes
his all on us—the sun, the moon, the stars, his very own Son. He

153

holds nothing back when it comes to giving. **When humankind first sinned, it was out of selfishness**, wanting to be more like God, taking instead of giving. Sin always has to do with serving self, not others. When we get outside of ourselves and focus on being conductors of stuff rather than collectors, we can start living a godly life—and imitating the perfect one.

So here's the golden question: if you were completely free from all worry about your needs and wants and had no desire for luxury and comfort, how different would your life be? When we start to Unstuff, life gains a new focus, and it isn't us. And with that perspective comes freedom—freedom from all the symptoms of stuffing and a new ability to practice multiplication rather than consumption.

> If you were completely free from all worry about your needs and wants and had no desire for luxury, how different would your life be?

Unstuffing Your Future

Are you serious about wanting a cure for stuff's control over your life? *ONLY TWO THINGS ARE REQUIRED: THE FAITH TO BELIEVE IN THE CURE, AND THE WILL TO WANT IT.* When Jesus worked his miracles here on earth, he repeatedly pointed out that it was the person's faith that had healed them. Faith is not the belief that *I can* but the belief that *God can*. And at the root of faith is the will. We can decide if we will let stuff control us or if we will choose to believe and act according to our faith.

> "God never intended that such a being as man should be the plaything of his feelings. The emotional life is a proper and

noble part of the total personality, but it is, by its very nature, of secondary importance. Religion lies in the will, and so does righteousness. The only good that God recognizes is a willed good; the only valid holiness is a willed holiness."
—A. W. Tozer

◆　◆　◆

If you're ready to take the next steps toward Unstuffing your future, here are seven things you can do today.

Avoid the Triggers

One of the biggest obstacles to multiplication is our incessant need for more, which gets fed by stuffing triggers.

Hayley

About six years ago I discovered an emotional trigger that left me feeling unfulfilled and wanting more stuff: my home decorating catalogs sent free of charge from my favorite stores. Just seeing the images of the perfect living room drove me crazy. I wanted all I saw but knew we couldn't afford it. The result of exposure to this trigger left me feeling impoverished and resentful. But lack of funds didn't stop me from acquiring more stuff—instead, it fueled me to try to get more for less. So I got creative and tried to find ways to reproduce my catalog scenes on the cheap. I was still practicing my stuffing while "saving money" at the same time! Five thousand dollars in credit card "savings" later, I decided I'd had enough and cleaned house. I quit opening the catalogs and sent them straight to the recycling pile. Slowly, thankfully, my desire for more diminished.

Triggers—those things that make us realize what we don't have and that drive us to want more—don't have to be a part of our lives anymore. **Each one of us has to find our own stuff triggers**, whether they're commercials, shows, certain people, magazines, or malls. It may be time to do a self-inventory—to take notice of how you feel and what you think after exposure to these triggers. If you watch an episode of *Desperate Housewives* and suddenly have to have a new Prada bag, you've found a trigger.

> "Temptation comes from our own desires, which entice us and drag us away. These desires give birth to sinful actions. And when sin is allowed to grow, it gives birth to death." JAMES 1:14-15

All the sins in our lives arise from our desires. And those desires are fed by our triggers—the things we look at, do, or think about that get us off track. In order to avoid these triggers, we need to have a clear exit strategy.

In order to Unstuff our lives and make more of an impact on the

Michael

My triggers are brand-new car lots and car collector magazines. Zero percent financing and lots of parking at our house are far too available for me, and I have to create barriers between me and a $40,000 impulse buy. Doesn't sound too appealing when I put it that way, does it? So one of the barriers I've constructed between my prospective idol and me is this: instead of accepting the salesman's $329 a month after trade-in option, I'll only allow myself to buy a car by paying cash in full. That barrier to instant gratification allows me to weather my weaker moments when the gleam of black pearl paint and polished chrome makes my heart race a tad too fast. Time for a cold shower. . . .

Michael I teach the men I mentor the "green bean method" for avoiding temptation in the supermarket and other public places. (Yes, we realize we have recurring green bean references in this book!) Here's how the GB method works: A guy catches a glance of an attractive woman, or even more subtle, hears the click of a woman's high-heeled shoes on the tile floor, and instead of succumbing to visual or audio triggers to check her out, he turns and grabs a can of green beans (or whatever is in the aisle) off the shelf and reads the label intently until the temptation passes. But these types of tips will never work if you aren't mindful of Christ and the power of Christ in you!

world for God's glory, we have to be smart about what we ingest with our eyes and chew on with our minds. A lot of the things we've allowed began with what seemed like harmless exposure to triggers. In order to Unstuff, we have to edit what we let our minds ponder.

> "The temptations in your life are no different from what others experience. And God is faithful. He will not allow the temptation to be more than you can stand. When you are tempted, he will show you a way out so that you can endure." 1 CORINTHIANS 10:13

Control Yourself

Since sin starts in our minds, it is crucial that we learn to take control of what we think. **One way we can take control of our thoughts is by reminding ourselves of the danger of letting our minds wander along the edges of sin.** After all,

TRIGGER CONTROL

Cancel the magazine subscriptions that trigger you to want more than you have.

Don't buy the quart of ice cream that will tempt you to eat it.

Avoid the store that most often causes you to buy "involuntary" stuff.

Look away when triggers tempt you.

Pray. When triggers can't be avoided, concentrate on God instead.

Get help. Have someone hold you accountable to your trigger exposure.

Reprogram. Start to replace your old actions with new, healthier ones.

---

it isn't only what we do that's sin; it's what we think as well. Notice Jesus' expansion of the definition of the sin of adultery: "You have heard the commandment that says, 'You must not commit adultery.' But I say, anyone who even looks at a woman with lust has already committed adultery with her in his heart" (Matthew 5:27-28). In Jesus' view, it's not only the physical act of adultery that's a sin; mental wanderings can be as well. That means that the thought, if allowed to fester in our minds and become more than a passing notion, turns into sin before we even do anything.

> "There is within the human heart a tough fibrous root of fallen life whose nature is to possess, always to possess. It covets 'things' with a deep and fierce passion." —A. W. Tozer

Of course, it has to be noted that temptation in itself is not a sin. If that were the case, we would have to say that Jesus sinned since he was tempted in the desert, and Scripture makes it clear that's not true. But a *TEMPTATION CAN TURN INTO SIN WHEN WE LINGER ON IT, PONDER IT, AND ULTIMATELY ACT ON IT.*

The alternative to a mind focused on sin is a mind that concentrates on whatever is pure and good. "Fix your thoughts on what is true, and honorable, and right, and pure, and lovely, and admirable. Think about things that are excellent and worthy of praise. Keep putting into practice all you learned and received from me—everything you heard from me and saw me doing. Then the God of peace will be with you" (Philippians 4:8-9). **In order to Unstuff our minds, we have to remove the influences of the world and replace them with the truth of God.**

Some practical ways to do this are through prayer, meditation, and thankfulness. Prayer is the fuel for self-control—it helps us to be mindful of what God wants from us. Meditation is just the act of thinking about God and his Word. It's the way we increase our understanding of truth—we think long and hard about what God's

Life on the Road, Day 90

Hayley: Today it occurred to me that I've been wearing the same outfit for seven days. And I love it! I used to think I needed to change every day and to look just so. After all, what would people say if I wore that same thing today that they saw me wear yesterday? Gasp! But on the road, I have no concern for those things. Wow, what is happening to me? And will it stick? My addiction to clothes is losing its appeal as we speak. And I love it! So does my pocketbook. Side note: Addy is missing her dog, cat, and grandma (who lives with us in Tennessee) terribly.

Word says and how it applies to our lives. Thankfulness is express-
ing our appreciation to God for who he is and what he has done
in our lives. ***We can't be thankful and bitter at the same
time.*** And we can't suffer from lack and be thankful at the same
time. Thankfulness is the weapon of choice for the person who
wants to Unstuff.

THANKFUL LIST

Having trouble keeping a grateful heart? Try writing it down.
Make a list of everything you are thankful for and then read it out
loud to yourself each morning and each evening. As you do, it
will become part of your heart and your mind, and gradually you
will find that you are able to focus on your abundance instead of
your lack.

Live within Your Means

If you spend more than you make, it's time to Unstuff.
Somewhere in your mind is the idea that you deserve something
that wasn't intended for you. That leads to a cluttered and bloated
life filled with stuff rather than faith and hope. But when we make
a conscious determination to live within our means, we move away
from the control of stuff.

How to Live within Your Means

Only pay cash. The easiest way to let your desire for more stuff get
out of control is to use plastic. It's so easy and painless to swipe
the card and hit Accept, but that ease makes it hard to say no to
your desires. So determine to live on cash alone. Then you can
decide how much you are going to spend when you are sober rather
than when you are drunk on shopping.

Buy pre-loved. There's nothing quite like the feeling of *new*. That
new-car smell is intoxicating, and new clothes make you feel like
a new person. We love new. But new can come with a heavy price
tag, and this addiction to new can quickly put us outside our
means. Not convinced that used is the way to go? Then consider
some of these ideas. In our "fleet" of cars, we have a Mercedes
S-Class and a BMW 540i that we bought used. New, these two
cars would have cost more than $85,000, but we got them for
$12,000 total. And in the process of writing this book, the S-Class
is now sold (still Unstuffing as we write!). That said, living with a
luxury car isn't reserved for the super wealthy; it can also be available to the super resourceful (at least those who don't mind a pre-
loved ride).

Rest

Does your life feel way too busy and out of whack? *BUSYNESS*
doesn't have to be an inevitable part of life—it **can be engi-
neered out of your daily patterns**. But first you have to
believe that (a) busyness is unnatural and unhealthy and (b) you
can change your habits by an act of your will.

Hayley

I used to be out of control when it came to grocery shopping. I shopped by sight: if it looked good, I bought it. We'd end up with cupboards bursting with food—a lot of which we never ate. But having a set amount of cash in my pocket each week forced me to be strategic about shopping and buy only what we would use that week. It has saved us a ton of money . . . and a ton of cupboard space!

When you take the time to think through what's important, you can find a way to get everything done that really needs to be done. **Letting things slide isn't the end of the world.** The question to ask is this: Is getting everything done leading me to sin? Is it causing me to stress or worry or to become bitter, resentful, or irritable? If so, something needs to change.

Rest isn't an illusion or reserved only for the privileged few, and it isn't some far-off promise waiting for you in

Hayley

I am a clothes addict. I like shopping, and I like expensive clothes. I used to shop at stores like Anthropologie and walk away with a shirt and pants for $150. Each time I did, it made me both intoxicated with that new-clothes high and sick with that new-clothes price. So in an attempt to Unstuff my life, I tried an experiment: to buy all my clothes at thrift stores. Let me tell you, it *can* be done. And it's amazing. In one trip to Goodwill, I bought twenty-three pieces of clothing for $16. And I'm talking all name-brand items—stylish and cute, just what I was looking for. The only thing I had to be willing to give up was the right to say, "I'm the first person to wear this." I calculated that to buy all those clothes new would have cost me $650. Now how's that for living within your means?

Hayley

I found that communication was a key part of setting me free from my busyness. With a full-time career as an author, publishing over four books a year; an active four-year-old daughter; and a home to keep, my time was often stretched thin. I constantly found myself in a frantic race to keep up with work, mothering, and housework. So in order to find the peace I needed, I sat down with Michael to talk about priorities. We talked about what was most important to us, what was most urgent, and what could slide if time got tight. In the end we created a priority list for the activities that consumed most of my hours day-to-day, and this is how it went:

> *Care for Addy*
> *Write*
> *Cook*
> *Clean*

This list helped me to see where most of my time went, and it also set me free to let anything after that slide depending on how the day was going. This released me from asking myself, *How can I possibly do all I have to do today?* It gave me permission to say, *Ignore that pile of laundry—you've got a book to work on or a game to play with Addy.*

retirement. Rest is possible every day, even in the midst of our work. And rest is necessary to the life of faith, because while busyness replaces relationship, rest paves the way for it.

"All who have entered into God's rest have rested from their labors, just as God did after creating the world. So let us do our best to enter that rest. But if we disobey God, as the people of Israel did, we will fall." HEBREWS 4:10-11

God wants us to rest—not to retire or become lazy, but to rest—so we won't allow our work or the stuff we work for to become more important than he is. ***REST IS REQUIRED OF THE BELIEVER FIRST BECAUSE IT IS IN IMITATION OF GOD, WHO RESTED ON THE SEVENTH DAY.*** Rest is also important because it's in this rest that we hear from God. When we're caught up in a flurry of activity and hurry, we can't hear his voice; we only hear the commands of the stuff that's yelling to get done. But when we rest, we take the yoke of Christ on ourselves and make him a part of our labor.

> Jesus said, "Come to me, all of you who are weary and carry heavy burdens, and I will give you rest. Take my yoke upon you. Let me teach you, because I am humble and gentle at heart, and you will find rest for your souls. For my yoke is easy to bear, and the burden I give you is light." MATTHEW 11:28-30

Life isn't meant to be a rat race where we run around aimlessly in search of stuff. It's intended to be a race toward the face of God,

IS YOUR LIFE TOO BUSY?

Make a list of everything on your day planner: work, soccer practice, worship team, planning committee, parenting, cleaning, dance class, study group—all the stuff that keeps you busy. Then pray about each item on the list and decide what can be cut in order to give you more time to rest from your labors and live for Christ. What are some things that complicate your life and cut into your time with family, friends, and the Father? Are there some things you need to start saying no to? If your priority list is set with God on top, family second, and work after that, it will be easier to make decisions about what stuff takes precedence. If any stuff in your life skews your priority list, it's time to Unstuff yourself.

Life on the Road, Day 105

Michael: One of the ways I promised to Unstuff was to lighten up about travel schedules—go, go, go, that sort of thing. Well, I'd say I've gotten better (?) at it since I had to fly the girls home as we passed the three-month mark and Addy was crying for home "right on schedule," starting at the ninety-day mark. On the bright side, I'm making awesome time. On the gloomy side, I've never been lonelier in my life. Me, the guy who loves being alone and needs his space. Go figure.

in which we realize that what really matters isn't the stuff around us but the God above us.

Practice Peace

Peace is taking a nap with a baby in your arms. It's leaving the office when there's more work to be done so you can watch your daughter's dance recital. It's spending an hour at the end of the day just talking with your spouse or a friend instead of doing what "needs" to be done. And **it's putting less focus on work and more on relationship**.

One of the best ways to gain peace is to practice what's called the "morning watch." *The morning is the firstfruits of the day—the beginning of everything—and it sets the pace for all that follows.* When the morning is dedicated to waiting on and watching for God in worship, prayer, and Bible study, the entire day is transformed. Our priorities fall into place, our heartbeats relax, and our troubles get addressed. The "morning watch" that lasts at least thirty minutes leads to a richer and more satisfying life because it gets us in sync with God's Spirit within us. And it gives us the energy to complete what needs to be completed in the hours ahead. When we start our day with the singular focus of watching to see what God wants us to do today, we are set free from the control of stuff and placed under the control of the Father.

When the morning is dedicated to waiting to hear from God and getting your orders for the day, the tone is set for a more peaceful day. But there will be times throughout the day when stress creeps in and threatens to steal that peace. When those moments come, **one of the best things to do is remember the word providence—God's hand in your life**. When the temperature rises and schedules get demanding, remind yourself, *God is in control of my day, and since I trust in his providence, I believe this interruption is for a greater purpose than I know*. When you gain the perspective that God is in control of your schedule, you can be set free from the demands put on you by other people and yourself. Nothing happens except what God has allowed to happen, and in that we can find peace. The next time life gets out of control, keep in mind that it's not out of his control, only yours.

Pray for Today

HOW MANY OF OUR PRAYERS ARE FOCUSED ON STUFF? Most of the prayers we pray for ourselves are about our stuff, and many of the prayers about the future are about stuff. "Please, Lord, give us that bigger house, better job, nicer car. Give us that friend, that part in the play, that parking space." So why not consider praying only for today: "Give us this day our daily bread" (Matthew 6:11, NKJV). Without concern for tomorrow, we can ask God to give what needs to be given today. And we can emphasize the needs of others over ourselves. When we change our prayers to reflect our desire to Unstuff our lives, our faith grows. And as our faith grows, our infatuation with stuff diminishes.

Give

> "One life wholly devoted to God is of more value to God than one hundred lives simply awakened by His Spirit."
> —OSWALD CHAMBERS

> Unstuffing means enriching others' lives by impoverishing your own.

The real beauty of the Unstuffed life is the amount of stuff that can be given to the needs of others. **When stuff no longer has a stranglehold on our lives, we are more free to share and to bring others into our abundance.** The more we Unstuff, the less life becomes about us and the more of an impact we have on the world around us.

As we grow in the practice of Unstuffing, God increases our capacity to give. As it says in 2 Corinthians 9:10, "He will provide and increase your resources and then produce a great harvest of generosity in you." *Generosity breeds multiplication.* How much more valuable is our stuff when it can bless not only us but many others?

Are you willing to enrich someone else's life if it means your own poverty? The widow with her two small coins gave away all she had in order to enrich the lives of others and to honor God (Luke 21:1-4). With that offering, she was left with absolutely nothing. And Jesus applauded her to his disciples. But when the rich man asked what he could do to serve God and Jesus told him to sell all he had and give the money to the poor, he was unable (Matthew 19:16-24).

When it comes to giving sacrificially, Christ is to be our example. He was rich, but he gave it all up in order to save us. Though he owned everything in heaven, he gave it all up to come to earth (2 Corinthians 8:9). It is only when God masters our wallets and our stuff that we can be true reflections of our Lord's generosity to a hungry world.

Your Own Multiplication Style

GIVING WITHOUT LOVE IS SPIRITUALLY WORTHLESS. In the words of Paul, "If I gave everything I have to the poor and even sacrificed my body, I could boast about it; but if I didn't love others, I would have gained nothing" (1 Corinthians 13:3). As we begin to Unstuff, our eyes become opened to the ways we can multiply what we've been given for the good of others. For many this has become a passion. We've met many believers who have made radical changes in their lives in order to Unstuff themselves and live generously.

Our friend Mike Foster, creator of *Junkycarclub.com*, has created a way for people to change the way they think about stuff by committing to get rid of expensive car payments and instead stick to good-old used cars. His pledge and the pledge of others in the club is to spend no more than five thousand dollars on the purchase of a car and to buy nothing newer than ten years old. After making a name for himself in the design world, he found himself falling in love with his luxury sports car, and this began to disturb him. When he realized how much of his cash and self-image he was putting into what he drove, he decided to make a change. So he sold his beauty and bought a car that ran but was often without heat and had a strange smell he couldn't quite peg. But the important thing isn't his suffering but his newfound ability to give what was his old car payment to Compassion International each month.

But you don't have to create a branded, marketed movement

surrounding your Unstuffing. You can just do it and blog about it. That's what old friends from Michael's college days are doing at ***www.anoregoncottage.com***. Brian and Jami moved their family from the big city to a rural area in Oregon and explore a life that is rich in the important things. They describe cottage living this way: **"A cottage can be anywhere or anything (condo, ranch, farmhouse) as long as you have the 'cottage mentality' of *living simply, loving imperfection, and making do or doing without.*** It's about cherishing the people in our lives and putting them before things." It's hard to argue with that! And while there might not be an obvious charity or organization that is benefiting from their Unstuffing, a closer look reveals that they are multiplying this lifestyle through their blog and, perhaps most important, through their children. To quote our daughter, they do what different does.

Whether you chose to Unstuff, declutter, free up more time, help others, or focus your worship on the One who deserves it, you'll no doubt have people tell you that the desire to pursue stuff is normal. *BUT YOU DON'T HAVE TO BE NORMAL! DO WHAT DIFFERENT DOES.*

When you spend your time and money on the things that really matter to God (himself and your neighbor), you stuff your life with things you can never buy: **love and grace.**

COMFO CLUTHE
MONEYSE
MONDAY NIGHT FOOTBA
JUNK MOTOR HO
SATION DER
SUBSCRIPTION
CLOSETS TIME-SHA
TION PANEL
SAFETY VACATION CA
SLEEP SKI BO
SSONS CREDIT CAR
URE FOOD
ES IA
IBLE STUDY ROMAN
CER PRACTIC
VIDEO GAMES
AMILY GAME CAR
UT EXERCISE IMA
JEWELRY SHOE
SION TWITTER GOSS
COUPONS MAGAZIN
OVIE STARS

NOTES

1. http://www.pointloma.edu/Assets/PLNU/Viewpoint/VP+American+ Consumption+Numbers+Winter+2009.pdf.

2. "Consumer Debt Statistics," Money-zine.com, http://www.money-zine.com/Financial-Planning/Debt-Consolidation/Consumer-Debt-Statistics.

3. "Do Not Mail: The Facts about Junk Mail," ForestEthics, http://www.donotmail.org/section.php?id=3.

4. "Majority of Christians Say Busyness Hinders Their Relationship with God," *Christianity Today Australia*, August 11, 2008, http://au.christiantoday.com/article/majority-of-christians-say-busyness-hinders-their-relationship-with-god/4055.htm.

5. Frank Newport, "Questions and Answers about Americans' Religion," December 24, 2007, http://www.gallup.com/poll/103459/questions-answers-about-americans-religion.aspx.

6. Nancy Shute, "Why Loneliness Is Bad for Your Health," *U.S. News & World Report*, November 12, 2008, http://health.usnews.com/health-news/family-health/brain-and-behavior/articles/2008/11/12/why-loneliness-is-bad-for-your-health.html; Mark Stibich, "How Do Relationships Improve Aging?" December 9, 2006, http://longevity.about.com/od/lifelongrelationships/f/relationships.htm.

7. Bernardo Carducci, "Shyness: The New Solution," *Psychology Today*, January 1, 2000, http://www.psychologytoday.com/articles/200001/shyness-the-new-solution?page=2.

8. "Majority of Christians Say Busyness Hinders Their Relationship with God," *Christianity Today Australia*, August 11, 2008, http://au.christiantoday.com/article/majority-of-christians-say-busyness-hinders-their-relationship-with-god/4055.htm.

unstuff.org

ABOUT THE AUTHORS

Hayley DiMarco is the best-selling author of more than forty books, including *Dateable*, *Marriable*, *Mean Girls*, and *The Woman of Mystery*. She spent the early part of her career working for a little shoe company called Nike in Portland, Oregon, and Thomas Nelson Publishing in Nashville, Tennessee.

In 2002 Hayley left Nelson and founded Hungry Planet, a company intensely focused on feeding the world's appetite for truth by producing books and new media, taking on issues of faith and life with a distinctly modern voice.

Shortly after founding Hungry Planet, Hayley successfully completed a nationwide executive search for someone to run the company so she could focus on writing. She describes her husband, Michael, as her most successful business acquisition! In addition to the ten books he has authored or coauthored, Michael is also the creative principal behind Hungry Planet Design, a studio responsible for the concepts, branding, and design surrounding Hungry Planet's award-winning books and other media.

Hayley and Michael are the proud parents of almost forty Hungry Planet books, including nineteen best sellers, five ECPA Christian Book Award finalists, two ECPA winners, and one amazing human, their daughter, Addison.

Find out more about Hungry Planet at www.hungryplanetbooks .com and www.hungryplanetdesign.com.

To join in on our journey of Unstuffing or to become an Unstuffer yourself, check out www.unstuff.org and follow our Unstuffing on Twitter:

Michael: twitter.com/dimarco
Hayley: twitter.com/hayleydimarco

unstuff.org

Hungry Planet

Feeding the world's appetite for truth.

- �֍ Nine straight titles on the CBA young adult bestseller list
- �֍ More than 800,000 books in print
- ✖ Three finalists and one winner of the ECPA Christian Book Awards

After all this and more, Hungry Planet has established itself as the leading provider of books for teens and not-yet-old adults. Dedicated to creating relevant, spiritually based books, Hungry Planet delivers honest, in-your-face truth and twenty-first-century application within a visually engaging package no reader can forget.

www.hungryplanetbooks.com

CP0308

From **Hungry Planet** and **Tyndale House Publishers**

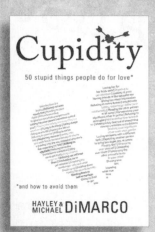

Cupidity: 50 Stupid Things People Do for Love and How to Avoid Them

You're a smart person. You really are. Most of the time. So why are you having such trouble making sense of your love life? Whether you're single or married, you might be surprised to discover that the answer lies in your own "Cupidity"—stupid love. In this book, popular authors Hayley and Michael DiMarco identify 50 of the most common acts of Cupidity, ways to avoid them and learn from them, and some surprising things God has to say about relationships. With the help of their inside information, you can find smart, successful love just around the corner.

978-1-4143-2467-8

The Woman of Mystery: Unveiling the Secret to True Romance

Hayley DiMarco employs her unique skill of tapping into her readers' deepest longings on a topic most women yearn for—romance. Women crave it in their relationships, their entertainment, and even their physical surroundings. In *The Woman of Mystery,* Hayley teaches women of all ages the secret of true romance and how it can lead to a life of peace and self-confidence in and beyond dating and marriage. You—and others—will notice an amazing difference in your thoughts, actions, words, and even your soul when you bring some mystery into your life.

978-1-4143-2468-5

unstuff.org